HUMAN CONSCIOUSNESS AND THE MATERIAL SOUL

The Consensus of Religion and Science

JOHN F. DEDEK

Volume XII: The Church and The World Series
Cyriac K. Pullapilly, General Editor
Saint Mary's College, Notre Dame, Indiana
George H. Williams, Consulting Editor
Harvard University

Cross Cultural Publications, Inc.

HUMAN CONSCIOUSNESS AND THE MATERIAL SOUL

The Consensus of Religion and Science

JOHN F. DEDEK

The Church and The World Series

Dedicated to the scholarly investigation of Christianity's interaction with the non-Christian world. This includes the Church's initial encounters with the civilizations of the ancient world, its influence on the tribal nationalities of the medieval times and its missinary impact in more modern times.Included also are Christianity's ideological and institutional impacts on the secular worlds of science, technology, politics, economics and the arts.

Authors who wish to publish in the series are requested to contact the General Editor at the address below.

Editorial Board:
Cyriac K. Pullapilly, General Editor
Saint Mary's College, Notre Dame, Indiana

George H. Williams, Consulting Editor
Harvard University

Printed in the United States of America. *First Edition*

Published by Cross Cultural Publications, Inc., Cross Roads Books
Library of Congress Catalogue Number: 2001 130397
ISBN: 0-940121-55-7

Contents

Foreword

This is a book that needed writing, and John Dedek has written it very well. After carefully tracing the idea of the spiritual soul through centuries of its Christian development, he brings it into conversation with contemporary neurobiology and cosmology. His point of beginning is the question: what is human consciousness? how does it function? where does it come from?

These are questions to which scientists have repeatedly turned their attention over the past fifteen years. One thing they agree upon, says Dedek: "The solution is something other than dualism, the theory that in man there is some interior spiritual substance, an immaterial soul, a ghost in the machine."

Is this viewpoint of contemporary science completely incompatible with the position taken in 1975 by the Congregation for the Doctrine of the Faith? In its letter "On Certain Questions Concerning Eschatology", it stated: "The church affirms that a spiritual element survives and subsists after death, an element endowed with consciousness and will, so that the 'human self' subsists. To designate this element the church uses the word 'soul'."

Later in the document the Congregation elaborates: "Christians must hold the two following essential points. On the one hand they must believe in the fundamental continuity, thanks to the power of the Holy Spirit, between our present life in Christ and the future life. On the other hand they must be clearly aware of the radical break between the present and the future one, due to the fact that the economy of faith will be replaced by the fullness of life."

Dedek would point out that the Congregation is concerned with the human person's survival after death. This fundamental continuity it attributes to the Holy Spirit. These concerns, he says, are quite compatible with the view of human consciousness held by contemporary science. To make his views clear, he shows the genesis and development of the idea of the "human soul" over the past two millennia.

This idea of a spiritual or immaterial soul, he notes, is entirely absent from scripture. It is the creation of early Christian thinkers like Origen and Augustine who used it to defend the freedom, intelligence and immortality of the human person. But contemporary Christian theology holds that "man is one being, a wholly material one." The immortality of the human person does not depend on his having a "spiritual soul".

Theology's encounter with science over the centuries has frequently been abrasive. In recent years, however, mutual suspicion has yielded to a new tentative conversation. Pope John Paul II gave the incipient dialogue solid support in his 1987 message: "If the cosmologies of the ancient Near Eastern world could have been purified and assimilated into the first chapters of Genesis, might contemporary cosmology have something to offer our reflections upon creation? Does an evolutionary perspective bring any light to bear upon theological anthropology, the meaning of the human person as the *imago Dei*, the problem of Christology, and even upon the development of doctrine itself? Can theological method fruitfully appropriate insights from scientific methodology and the philosophy of science?

"Science can purify religion from error and superstition; religion can purify science from idolatry and false absolutism. Each can draw the other into a wide world in which both can flourish."

Fittingly enough John Dedek gets his bearings for his own dialogue with science from Vatican II's Decree on Ecumenism: "In comparing doctrines they should remember that there exists a hierarchy of truths of Catholic doctrine, since their relationship to the fundamentals of Christian faith is diverse."

Theologian Kenan Osborne notes the three major categories within this hierarchy: solemn and official teachings of the church, undefined but official teachings of popes and bishops, and acceptable theological opinions. Situating the "spirituality of the soul" accurately within this triangle is the book's major theological task. It is an exercise in theological hermeneutics.

Francis Sullivan, S.J., notes that theology is an essentially hermeneutic endeavor. Hermeneutics is the science of interpretation. As an historical religion Christianity relies heavily on written documents from the past: scripture, the writings of the fathers, conciliar texts. Since scripture is the normative text, the interpretation of scripture is crucial. The science of hermeneutics was developed to aid this interpretive process. In recent years, however, scholars have learned how necessary it is to apply these same principles to the other texts, especially conciliar documents.

This new hermeneutic is crucial to addressing the question of the spirituality of the soul. As a theologian reads the documents of councils and commissions, it is imperative to understand their cultural context, the intentions of the authors, and the language they use. All are relevant to understanding the doctrinal statements and the place they occupy in the hierarchy of truth. This interpretative exercise forms the major part of the book's theological agenda.

If the church's major concerns are the survivability and continuity of the human person, can these concerns only be met by postulating a spiritual soul? The Congregation's appeal to the Holy Spirit to effect these ends would seem to open the way to a discussion of alternative possibilities. Dedek speaks of these as he reviews the work of contemporary theologians.

How then do we respond to the question asked by contemporary science: What is consciousness and how does it arise? Dedek does not pretend to have the answer. Nor does any one else at the present time. He does insist, however, that the answer will not lie in showing how an immaterial soul interacts with a material brain.

In what may be his most provocative suggestion, the author suggests that we explore more fully an equally significant question: What is matter? The tentative answers of contemporary science are tantalizing. As physicists and cosmologists have pushed the boundaries of human thought back to the "beginning" they have searched for a "unified field theory", a single theory compatible with relativity and quantum mechanics. A promising theory today is the String Theory.

Immensely over simplified it tells us that matter and energy are manifestations of differently vibrating "strings" that are the fundamental components of everything that is. As this new universe unfolds under the tentative probing of contemporary science, "matter" takes on a mystery and beauty that nearly defies imagining.

The author has done us a service by suggesting that theologians look for alternatives that adequately meet the church's old concerns even as they allow our religious consciousness to expand. As Pope John Paul said, religion and science can draw one another into a wider world where each can flourish.

George J. Dyer
Chicago Studies

Acknowledgements

Grateful acknowledgement is made for permission from Basic Books to reprint an excerpt from the copyrighted work, *A Universe of Consciousness: How Matter Becomes Imagination* by Gerald M. Edelman and Giulio Tononi (Basic Books, 2000), and to Harcourt Brace and Company for permission to reprint an excerpt from the copyrighted work, *The Feeling of What Happens: Body and Emotion in the Making of Consciousness* by Antonio Damasio (Harcourt Brace & Company, 1999).

Part One

Scientific Monism

Chapter One

State of the Question

In April of 1963 Richard P. Feynman gave three lectures on the impact of science on politics and religion as part of the John Danz Lecture Series at the University of Washington in Seattle. He began by saying, "In talking about the impact of ideas in one field on ideas in another field, one is always apt to make a fool of oneself. In these days of specialization there are too few people who have such a deep understanding of two departments of our knowledge that they do not make a fool of themselves in one or the other." Feynman did not take his own advice, and his lectures were brilliant.

But it is good advice for me, and I am going to follow it. I certainly am not going to try to solve the problem of consciousness, which in the past ten or fifteen years has been challenging the best scientists of our time. Nor am I going to try to evaluate any of the theories or hypotheses advanced by any of these men.

What I propose to do first is accept as true the consensus of nearly all the expert writers on this problem today. Although the problem of consciousness is not solved yet, one thing is certain and universally held: the solution is something other than dualism, the theory that in man there is some interior spiritual substance, an immaterial soul or, as Gilbert Ryle once called it, a "ghost in the machine". The true, albeit elusive, solution is natural and entirely physical.[1]

Then to set the stage for the theological analysis that will follow and which is the whole reason for this essay I will outline, as accurately as I can, the theories of three of the most recent and distinguished writers on the topic: 1) Colin McGinn, Philosopher, 2) Robert Penrose, Physicist and Mathematician, and 3) Antonio Damasio, Neurobiologist.

There have been philosophers, from the time of ancient Greece to the time of the enlightenment, who argue that there was in man no spiritual soul, free will, or the capacity to know that he can know. The problems that they were dealing with were analogous to what we are studying now. But they were dealing with these problems in their own context, for their own purposes, and with their own very limited knowledge about man. Besides, our theological purpose is a narrow one and will be served by focusing on the contemporary discussion about the origin of consciousness in human beings.

In the seventeenth century Robert Boyle, the "father of modern chemistry", vigorously protested the traditional union of chemistry with alchemy. But he unabashedly explained that while matter was corpuscular, it owed its inherent powers and motion ultimately to God, spirits or some other unknown forces beyond reason. A hundred years later Joseph Priestly had no tolerance for a "God of the gaps" as a rational scientific explanation of things that we do not understand. In the future, he said, scientists will explain nothing by spirits. All explanations will be sought in nature. In his enthusiasm Priestly ordered the clergy to drop the term *spirit* from their vocabulary. That, of course, was none of his business, but the reason he gave was a good one. Christianity, he said, has been corrupted by Platonism.

Priestly was not the first or the most violent critic of the introduction of Greek philosophy into Christianity. Some of the early Fathers like Tertullian were fiercely opposed to efforts by Augustine in the West and Origen in the East to mix neoplatonism with Christian doctrine and to interpret the bible through the eyes of Plotinus.

But in an effort to protect Christian beliefs about human intelligence (limited as it is), human freedom (limited as it is), and human immortality some influential patristic writers like Origen and Augustine introduced into Christian doctrine the Platonic idea of a spiritual or immaterial soul, an idea which was not contained in either the bible or the ancient creeds.

As a consequence, the "Christian" anthropology found today in many of our mediocre religious instruction books and frequently in popular preaching is really rooted in the teaching of Plato. Plato in the fifth century b.c. and Plotinus and neoplatonists in the third century a.d. taught that man is essentially inhabiting a material body. Many ordinary Christian people today, therefore, believe that the central teaching of the New Testament is about saving one's soul in this life so that one can go to heaven and live with God forever in the next life. As a result, many contemporary scientists and philosophers believe that Christian anthropology is dualistic. As we shall see in these pages both of these beliefs are mistaken.

I have divided this essay into two parts, a brief one called *scientific monism* and a longer section called *theological monism*. In both parts I am referring to the nature only of man, not of being. Universal monism—the theory that matter and being are synonymous so that nothing exists or can exist besides matter—is, at least as a strictly scientific tenet, impossible.

The natural empirical sciences as such are unable to demonstrate that there is not and cannot be a spiritual entity such as God. Science is properly agnostic about such matters, but it cannot be atheistic and still remain simply empirical science. There are certainly atheistic scientists around today, but they are not atheists inasmuch as they are scientists. They are atheists because they are men who for other than strictly empirical reasons have decided for an atheistic interpretation of reality.

In the second part I speak of theological monism. Again I say this in reference to man alone, not of all reality. (I am not a pantheist nor a remnant of the "death-of-God theologians" out of the nineteen sixties.) What I am saying is that Christian theology is not willing to describe man as an immaterial soul in a material body from which she is set free at death.

Plato and Descartes have done some mischief to theological thinking over the centuries, but dualism has not won the day. Rather contemporary Christian theology says that man is one being, a wholly material one. This statement is deeply rooted in the Old and New Testaments and Christian history. The "spirituality of the soul" has gotten tangled up at times with the immortality of man. But there is no necessary connection between the two, and in Christian history they frequently were not connected.

I do not know what the ultimate answer will be to the question, *What is Consciousness and How Does It Arise*? (or even if a final answer will ever be found). But I am sure that it will not be found by trying to determine how an immaterial mind can interact with a material brain.

The ultimate solution should be sought, I believe, solely in matter and probably will need a deeper answer to the question, *What is Matter*? (and perhaps deeper answers to related questions such as, What is Time and What is Space?). For a clear and current explanation of some of the possibilities here see Brian Greene's book, *The Elegant Universe: Superstrings, Hidden Dimensions, and the Quest for the Ultimate Theory.*[2]

Chapter Two

Three Current Responses

Colin McGinn

Colin McGinn, Professor of Philosophy at Rutgers University, has written five books and many articles on human consciousness.[1] The least technical and his most recent book is entitled *The Mysterious Flame: Conscious Minds in a Material World.*[2] A brief summary of this book follows.

Consciousness is not simply wakefulness or self-awareness. It is the actual experiencing of sensations, emotions, feelings, thoughts. To a limited degree it can exist in babies and some animals. The brain is the seat, or better the womb, of consciousness. There is a bond or connection between the brain and the mind. What exactly this bond is is a deep mystery. In fact, it is an ultimate mystery, one that never will be unraveled.

There are two customary and competing explanations of the connection between the brain and the mind—materialism and dualism. But neither is useful. Materialism reduces the mind to neurons and electrochemical activity among them. The electrochemical antics in the neurons do not cause consciousness. They *are* consciousness. Anything more we might think is consciousness is in fact an illusion, an error of perception.

Dualism, on the other hand, separates mind from matter. The brain and the mind are different things. They exist together, work together, but are essentially different. In fact disembodiment of the mind is possible. It is like a "ghost in the machine".

A new and better idea is to say that consciousness depends on an unknowable natural property of the brain. This property is not merely the electrochemical processes. It is not merely some other presently unknown property. It is not a supernatural or purely spiritual property. It is some natural property which explains how consciousness emerges from brain tissue. McGinn proposes that we call this property C*.

This property (C*) is not knowable by our human minds. Introspection can make us aware of consciousness inwardly. But it cannot tell us how it arises from any properties of the brain. And empirical observation can let us see microscopically inside the crevices of the cortex or any part of the brain. But it cannot see consciousness. McGinn summarizes the argument in this way.

> At root, the reason we cannot solve the mind-body problem is that we cannot *see* the mind. Nature has equipped us with self-awareness so that we can know what is going on in us mentally, and it has equipped us with five senses so that se can detect what is going on in the spatial world around us. But these cognitive faculties are not designed to fathom what *links* mind to brain.

However, the fact that we cannot explain how consciousness arises from brain tissue means only that it is something mysterious. It does not mean that it is something supernatural or miraculous.

In a later chapter called "Mind Space" McGinn raises a surprising question. He begins by arguing that everything in the world is spatial, existing and occupying space—everything, that is, except consciousness. All the objects of consciousness are spatial but not consciousness itself. For instance, my visual experience of red or my emotion of fear are not solid things that take up any space, unless one insists that consciousness and the physical brain are identical and therefore commensurate. Here McGinn raises his surprising question. Instead of conceding that the mind is really spatial, why not inquire whether the brain is non-spatial?

McGinn is curious to know what existed before the Big Bang, before matter was created and with it space. The pre-Big Bang universe was not spatial because space came into being with matter. Perhaps, he speculates, "mind is an aspect of matter but an aspect which does not fit the usual conception of matter". That is to say, it is an aspect of matter which entails some kind of pre-Big Bang non spatiality.

Since the common theory of cosmologists today is that matter, space and time all came into existence together at the Big Bang, McGinn acknowledges that he is not saying that this theory is true, only that it is a "daring speculation" which might be considered in an area as mysterious as consciousness.

What is Space? is not a question to which contemporary physics can give a complete and final answer. Despite appearances, space is curved; and there may be more spatial dimensions than three, more total spaces than the one we exist in, and perhaps "non locality effects" by non local causal agents. Perhaps space also will prove to be mysterious. At least there is still some work to be done in physics here.

Galen Strawson, a fellow of Jesus College, Oxford, and author of *Mental Reality*, in the July 11, 1999 issue of the *New York Times Book Review* applauds *The Mysterious Flame* for its clarity and accuracy and says that he knows of no better introduction to the problem of consciousness than this. He congratulates McGinn for seeing "that there must be something deficient in our idea of space, as well as matter." In fact, Strawson says, the reason we find consciousness so mysterious is that we have such a bad picture of matter. The answer to the mind/brain problem lies somewhere in the answer to the question: What is matter?

Strawson says:

> . . . it has been a long time since the 18th century philosopher-chemist Joseph Priestly pointed out that there are no scientific grounds for supposing that the fundamental constituents of matter have any truly solid central part, and the picture of grainy, inert particles has effectively disappeared in the strangeness of modern quantum theory and superstring theory.

Modern physics understands matter not as some kind of solid stuff but as forces, energy and fields. Consciousness also might easily be thought of as a result of energy, a kind of force or even as a kind of field. At least consciousness and matter are not as disparate as it might at first seem. What we have to do is start with a better definition of matter.

Roger Penrose

Strawson, I believe, points the inquiry in the right direction, and that direction has been taken by Oxford physicist and mathematician Roger Penrose.[3] Roger Penrose is reluctant to define *consciousness*. The reason for his reluctance, he says, is that at the present state of the argument we do not know what it is, and so if we were to define it now we probably would define the wrong thing. However we can describe it to some extent. Consciousness includes things like perceptions of color and harmonies, memory, free will and the actions it controls, understanding or insight, awareness and intelligence. Besides, he notes, as a mathematician he is usually comfortable enough if he can explain the connections between things without ever defining them.

Since Isaac Newton, physics has taken some giant steps forward. Take, for instance, quantum theory and the two theories of relativity. They are internally coherent and empirically verified. But general relativity and quantum mechanics are not compatible with each other in our present state of understanding. There is a missing theory, a theory that we still do not have, explaining the union or connection between the theory of general relativity and quantum theory. Perhaps, Penrose says, it will be in this missing link that we will discover the explanation of consciousness.

Quantum mechanics is clear, coherent and empirically verified. Nonetheless it also contains things that are still mysterious to us. Some of these mysteries are simply "puzzling"; others are "paradoxical."

Puzzling mysteries are about phenomena that are in fact real, part of physical nature, but still puzzling to us. Examples are called "wave-particle duality", "null measurements", "spin", and "quantum non locality or entanglement". Paradoxical mysteries, on the other hand, are signs that there is something wrong with the theory. Examples are often referred to as the "measurement problem" or "Schrödinger's cat" phenomenon. It is obviously important that we distinguish between these two types of mysteries as it is that we distinguish between true and false.

At this point Penrose introduces the mind-body problem, saying that there is a "fundamental problem with the idea that mentality arises out of physicality".

Penrose explains:

> The things we talk about in physics are matter, physical things, massive objects, particles, space, time, energy and so on. How could our feelings, our perception of redness, or of happiness have anything to do with physics? I regard this as a mystery.

Consciousness belongs to the mental world, and in this connection one often hears words like *soul*, *spirit*, *religion*. But this is a mystery of science, and people today prefer scientific explanations for things. However, it will be a challenge to provide one.

Mental activity cannot be reduced to computation. It includes more than what can be accomplished by an artificial intelligence like a computer. Penrose knows that there are people who dispute this, but he argues vigorously and persuasively against them.[4]

Penrose separates some differing opinions here. One is that awareness probably cannot be explained in physical, computational or any other scientific terms. Another is that all thinking is in the last analysis computational, and a sense of awareness is evoked simply in doing the computations. Another, which is Penrose's opinion, is that all physical action of the brain is not in the last analysis computational. There also is physical action of the brain that is not computational, and it is this physical action that somehow stimulates awareness.

Exactly how does it do this? Penrose's response is that the precise answer is not available in known physics. Our present understanding of physics at the quantum level is incomplete. There is something missing. It is possible that we may discover in that area the physical non computational activity of the brain that stimulates consciousness. ". . . not only do we need a new physics, but we also need a new physics which is relevant to the action of the brain." Perhaps we will find it someday, he suggests, in "a new quantum gravity theory". He also speculates that this new theory, with the support of a new non-local mathematics, might include a more intelligible "quantum non-local theory".

Antonio Damasio

A different approach to the issue of consciousness is taken by the neuroscientist, Antonio Damasio, M. W. Van Allen Distinguished Professor and Head of the Department of Neurology at the University of Iowa College of Medicine in Iowa City, in his book *The Feeling of What Happens: Body and Emotion in the Making of Consciousness*.[5]

Damasio admires the approach of Penrose who is seeing the "physical basis of the qualia problem" of consciousness, which usually is described by him simply as consciousness in general, whereas Damasio here is focusing on another part of the problem, namely the biological basis of the mental process.

One of the problems in the study of consciousness today is that the word *consciousness* is not defined by everyone univocally. Another problem is that some philosophers and scientists think that in human consciousness evolution has reached its peak. So they stand in awe of it, thinking that its reflex comprehension is out of our reach. Or they may think that it is too interior and private a matter to be studied scientifically. Others have become impatient with the problem, saying that consciousness is already perfectly understood or that the problem does not exist at all. Damasio himself believes that the problem of consciousness is a real one, that it will be with us for some time but can be broken up into parts and eventually solved scientifically.

The power of Damasio's book lies in its clinical, analytic, scientific and personal detail. It is impossible, of course, to capture the beauty and persuasiveness of his story in a summary as abbreviated as this. All we can hope for here is a thematic outline of some of his main conclusions and leave the rest behind for the reader to enjoy alone.

From the perspective of neurobiology the problem that consciousness presents can be put into two interrelated questions: 1) How does the brain engender the mental patterns or images of an object, and 2) How does the brain at the same time also engender a sense of self in the act of knowing an object. Damasio does not hope to solve this problem once and for all here, only to contribute some ideas from a biological perspective to its eventual clarification in a collaborative effort with other scientists.

It will be helpful at the start to distinguish "core consciousness" and "extended consciousness". Core consciousness is simple and is not specifically human. It gives the organism a sense of self here and now, in this instant and in this space. It does not need memory, reason or language, and does not envision a future or recall a past. Accordingly it effects in an organism only a "core self".

"Extended consciousness", on the other hand, is more complex, in some instances far more complex and at simple levels may exist in nonhuman organisms. It provides an organism with an elaborate sense of self, an "autobiographical self", an identity as a person with a history, with a past and a future. It depends on memory and is enhanced by language.

In Damasio's theory, stripped bare, the first condition of consciousness, what makes it possible, is the existence of a "proto-self". The proto-self is not some kind of homunculus inside the brain (another mind in the mind of the body). Rather it is a preconscious biological antecedent of core consciousness, that is a "coherent collection of neural patterns which map, moment by moment, the state of the physical structure of the organism in its many dimensions."

Although the human body is continuously changing from conception until death, there is a resolute permanence in its structure and operations. Within the organism there is an internal disposition toward stability which is necessary to maintain the life of the organism. As Damasio puts it, ". . . although the building blocks for the construction of our organisms are regularly replaced, the architectural designs for the varied structures of our organisms are carefully maintained."

The image projected by the body (e.g. its internal milieu, viscera, vestibular system, musculoskeletal frame) is one of stability, permanence, sameness, identity. The proto-self perceives nothing, knows nothing, is not conscious in any sense, and is not located in some region or regions of the brain. It is simply "a product of the interactions of neural and chemical signals among a set of regions". This may be "the blueprint and anchor" for what eventually may become or appear to be a self in the mind.

Psychology today is pretty well informed about the biological or neural process in which an object is perceived in the senses and known in the brain. Core consciousness arises when the object known, the organ knowing and the relation between the two are re-represented.

The first wordless knowing of something, either inside the organism like pain or outside it like a landscape, either from a new perception or from a memory, is accompanied by a feeling of knowing.

In the nonverbal act of knowing something the brain nonverbally perceived a change in the proto-self, and immediately on a second level it nonverbally catches itself undergoing this change. In other words, Damasio explains: "Core consciousness occurs when the brain's representation devices generate an imaged nonverbal account of how the organism's own state is affected by the organism's processing of an object, and when this process enhances the image of the causative object, thus placing it saliently in a spatial and temporal context."

The nonverbal story is this. The stable proto-self is represented to the brain. In the act of knowing an object the proto-self is changed and on a second level knows this. It is in the very act of representing its own changing state as it represents something else that the self becomes knowable. And so in that process core consciousness is created.

Once we understand the process by which the core self is created it is easy to see that repetition of the momentary sense of self can gradually create a more or less permanent or stable self-awareness and that a continuous repetition coupled with memory and enhanced by language can give rise to "extended consciousness". Thus ultimately the autobiographical self comes into being.

For the sake of the record and his colleagues Professor Damasio sums up his theory in more technical and exact language. It might be useful to some readers to quote it here:

> The hypothesis states that core consciousness occurs when the brain forms an imaged, nonverbal, second order account of how the organism is causally affected by the processing of an object. The imaged account is based on second-order neural patterns generated from structures capable of receiving signals from other maps which represent both the organism (the proto-self) and the object. The assembly of second-order neural patterns describing the object-organism relationship modulates the neural patterns which describe the object and leads to the enhancement of the image of the object. The comprehensive sense of self in the act of knowing an object emerges from the contents of the imaged account, *and* from the enhancement of the object, presumably in the form of a large-scale pattern that combines both components in a coherent manner.
>
> The neuroanatomical structures required by the hypothesis encompass those that support the proto-self; those needed to process the object; those needed to generate the imaged account of the relationship and to produce its consequences. The neuroanatomy underlying the processes behind the proto-self and object . . . includes brain-stem nuclei, the hypothalamus, and somatosensory cortices. The neuro-anatomy underlying the imaged account of the relationship and the enhancement of object image . . . includes the cingulate cortices, the thalamus, and the superior colliculi. The subsequent image enhancement is achieved via modulation from basal forebrain/brain-stem acetylcholine and monoamine nuclei as well as from thalamocortical modulation.

In conclusion, we should note that in Damasio's mind the genesis of core consciousness is the greatest mystery. But extended consciousness with the emergence of the autobiographical self is not, as many people would think, the greatest glory of man. It is, of course, a magnificent emergent, one that sets man apart from all other creatures on this planet. But more magnificent for Damasio is conscience, which creates law and ethics to govern man's social and interpersonal affairs. It is only after consciousness that conscience emerges.

Summary of Part One

Colin McGinn sees the mind-body problem as a mystery, one that might never by totally understood. He does not say this because he secretly thinks that there is something spiritual or supernatural at work here, but simply because the mind may not be equipped to penetrate this area.

Roger Penrose also sees the problem as a mystery, one that will not be solved until we discover a new physics which is relevant to the activity of the brain. The needed but missing physics may lie in a new theory of quantum gravity, a new understanding of matter at the quantum level of things.

And Antonio Damasio also thinks that we are dealing with a deep mystery. But as a serious contribution he outlines an imaginative and credible theory of core consciousness arising naturally out of the brain's awareness of the changes that occur in the organism or the "proto-self" when the brain knows some object. Eventually repetition, memory and finally language enhance and develop core consciousness into extended consciousness and a "biographical self".

Like their colleagues these three experts—a philosopher, physicist/mathematician, and neurobiologist—are at once modest and consistent in seeking a solution in nature, not in some supernatural force or spiritual being that we cannot experience, test or see. Unlike Robert Boyle they do not appeal to the "God of the gaps" or to a ghost hiding in the machine. They humbly work on, hoping to find a natural solution to a problem which at the present is clouded in some mystery.

Part Two

Theological Monism

Chapter Three

The Christian Sources

A Preliminary Note on Methodology

A theologian's purpose is not to create a new and better religion than the one he has inherited. Of course, if he believes that it is fundamentally false he is obligated to abandon it. If not, his specific task as a theologian is to define it, that is to identify exactly what its nature is, what are its foundations and its essential tenets and practices. Secondly, his task is to explicate what is latent in its essence but not at present apparent. Thirdly, his job is to propose ways that the religion can be changed, modified, enhanced or updated, so that it will be a more useful religion for men without destroying its essence.

Once one thinks about this job description he will realize that it is what Peter Drucker would describe as a widow-maker.[1] It is at least a task that frequently has ended in failure. Think for instance of the many divisions that exist within Christianity today and have been caused at least partly by theologians trying to do a theologian's job.

A sure way to fail is to simply speculate in the abstract on what is a better idea than an earlier one, more suitable in our contemporary culture or seems more reasonable in itself. These are not bad questions in themselves and need to be asked. But they need to be asked in the context of the origin and history of the religion that one is studying. Unless one is persuaded that the foundations of the religion are wobbly, the theologian needs to study new questions in the context of the religion's tradition.

That is what we propose to do in this section. We are going to inquire: where does the doctrine of the spirituality of the soul fit in the Christian religious tradition? The answer to this question will make clear the Christian presumption or bias on the scientific question about the genesis and nature of human consciousness.

Anthropology in the New Testament

A kind of dualism already exists in the writings of Plato. But a more recent and familiar form comes from the seventeenth century philosopher, Rene Descartes. Descartes believed that man is made up of two distinct substances, one a material body and the other an immaterial or spiritual soul.

According to this philosophical theory, I am an immaterial soul who has a material body which I use for a time. Descartes offered no clear explanation of how these two distinct substances work together. This view of man has been perhaps oversimplified but tersely summed up, first by Gilbert Ryle and afterwards by many other philosophers and scientists, as the doctrine of "the ghost in the machine".

Unfortunately this is the understanding of man that is currently found in popular preaching and catechisms and is widely believed by many Christians today. The basic doctrine is this: Man is a combination of a material body and an immaterial soul. When he dies his body decays and turns to ashes, and his soul goes to its individual judgment before God. If this judgment is favorable, his soul goes to heaven, perhaps with a slight detour to purgatory. If not the soul goes to hell.

At the end of the world the body of every human being rises from the dead and is rejoined to its spiritual soul. Then there is a "general judgment" in which everyone is publicly judged and then goes to a final and eternal reward or punishment. But that is not the anthropology that is found in the New Testament of in any of the ancient creeds.

In the Hebrew Old Testament the word *soul* usually designates an individual person (e.g. Gen. 2, 7; Gen. 46. 18); sometimes it means the life principle (e.g. Exech. 37, 10; Judg. 5, 18). But Hebrews *were* living bodies; they did not have living bodies. However, the Book of Wisdom (which is not found in the Hebrew bible but only in the Greek Septuagint and was probably originally written in Greek in the last half of the first century b. c.) may have imported a kind of dualism of body and soul from ancient Greek ideas of soul. Wisdom 9, 15 reads, ". . . a perishable body weighs down the soul, and its earthly tent burdens the thoughtful mind." This verse is reminiscent of Plato (*Phaedo* 81c), but its meaning most likely is simply that our deliberations are weak and earthbound because of the body and its concerns.

English bibles customarily translate the Hebrew word נֶבֶשׁ (nepeš) as "soul". This can be misleading. For *soul* suggests ideas that go back to Greek philosophy and medieval scholasticism, where it is understood as some kind of subsistent form. The Hebrew word *nepes* suggest nothing of the sort. *Nepes* designates man in his total essence, a psycho-physical totality in his concrete existence. It is useful to note this, because the New Testament, which uses the Greek word *psyche* which is translated as "soul", shows a heavy dependence on the Old Testament, not on Greek philosophy.

The reader today, who may have been influenced by Greek philosophy either directly or by way of medieval scholasticism, must be careful not to read Greek concepts into this literature. Although it was written in the Greek language, it was written by Hebrews and reflects the Hebrew tradition and mentality. The New Testament uses the Greek word *psyche* instead of the Hebrew word *nepes*. But it keeps the same basic meaning.

In the four gospels *soul* refers to one's life, the whole person or the self. Some examples are: Luke 12, 20; Luke 12, 22; Matt. 2, 20; Matt. 2, 28; Matt. 6, 25; Mark 3, 4; Mark 10, 45; John 10, 11; John 13, 37; John 15, 13-17. This usage is the same in Luke's Acts of the Apostles for instance: Acts 2, 4, 43 and Acts 3, 23. The word *soul* is also used as the locus of feeling and emotion, for instance: Matt. 22, 37; Matt. 26, 38; Mark 12, 30; Mark 14, 34; Luke 1, 46; Luke 2, 35; Luke 10, 27; Luke 12, 19; John 12, 27; Acts 4, 32; Acts 15, 24. In these passages the New Testament shows no difference from the Old Testament in its use of the word *soul*.

There are some texts, however, when the author uses the word *psyche* not merely in a secular sense but with a new and special meaning as the subject of a new supernatural life, that is a new relationship with God bestowed on him freely by God, and as the object of salvation by God through Jesus, for instance, in Matt. 10, 39 the author says that men can kill the body but they cannot kill the psyche; God, however, can kill both. Here *soul* designates not natural life but the new supernatural life of the Christian. The same is true in Matt. 16, 26; Mark 8, 36; Heb. 10, 39; Jas. 1, 21; 1 Peter 1, 9.

The psyche appears as the object of supernatural salvation and pastoral care in Matt. 11, 29; 1 Peter 1, 22; 1 Peter 2, 25; 1 Peter 4, 19. One does not detect the footprints of Plato or any other dualist here, only a new Christian doctrine of man's new relationship to God in grace. Like *nepes* in the Old Testament *psyche* in the New signifies the totality of self, and in some texts in the New Testament it is put in the context of the radically new idea of divine adoption and eternal salvation of the total self.

In the epistles St. Paul does not describe human being as such. Rather he is concerned about the relations of human beings to God and to the world. Describing these aspects of a human being Paul uses a variety of Greek words—σῶμα (body), σάρξ (flesh), πψχή (soul), πνεῦμα (spirit), νοῦς (mind), kardía (heart).

Paul uses the word *psyche* (soul) in the same sense as the Hebrew word *nepes* to designate a living being, a person with vitality, freedom and intelligence, a self with purely natural life (not dominated by the Spirit of God). Some examples of this are found in 1 Cor. 15, 4-5; 2 Cor. 1, 23; 2 Cor. 12, 15; 1 Thes, 28; Phlm. 2, 30; Rom. 11, 3; Rom. 13, 1.

Nous (mind) names man in his capacity to know and understand. Check, for instance, Rom. 1, 20 and Rom. 7, 23. It has practically the same meaning for Paul as *kardia* (heart). The only difference is that *kardia* connotes the more passionate aspect of the intelligent self. See as examples 2 Cor. 2, 4; 2 Cor. 3, 14; 2 Cor. 7, 3; 2 Cor. 8, 16; Rom. 1, 24; Rom. 9, 2; Rom. 10, 6-10.

For St. Paul *soma* (body) is the visible tangible aspect of man, as is found in Rom. 12, 4; 1 Cor. 12, 14-26; 2 Cor. 12, 2-3. But a human being does not just have a *soma*: he is a *soma*. *Soma* is the same thing as a whole living organism, a self, a person, as is clear in Rom. 6, 12-13; Rom. 8, 13; Rom. 1, 1; 1 Cor. 9, 27; Phil 1, 20. It is similar to English usage where *somebody* and *someone* designate the same thing.

Occasionally Paul uses *soma* pejoratively to signify the natural man ruled by sin before being set free by Christ (e.g. Rom. 6, 6; Rom. 7, 14-23), but typically he uses the word *sarx* (flesh) to name the natural man left to his own powers, weak and earthbound (e.g. Rom. 8, 5-8; Gal. 6, 19-21); this is meant to contrast him from the man who is under the influence of the spirit of God (e.g. Rom. 8, 4-13; Gal. 3, 3; Gal. 4, 29). Also, in 2 Cor. 5, 2-10 (as in 2 Pet. 1, 13-15) the author looks forward to his death so as to be with God. But to read this, as some have done, as evidence that the soul can have a separate existence from the body stretches the meaning of the text as well as the entire New Testament context in which it appears.

Pneuma (spirit) is often used by Paul in this connection as an antithesis to *sarx* (flesh). In the New Testament the precise definition of *pneuma* is difficult to pin down. In general it is the power of God which comes from outside of man. It is not the same as *psyche* or soul which is natural to man. It is rather a gift of God which goes beyond men's natural powers, especially as they are influenced by the flesh and insofar as they are ready to receive the spirit of God.

Therefore, a mind/body problem does not exist in the bible, Old Testament or New. The sacred writers knew nothing of dualism, Platonic or Cartesian. They knew nothing of, never envisioned, bodies living without souls or souls living without bodies. They knew only living human beings who were not bodies having souls or souls having bodies. They were units, each a single thing, one unified living self.

As far as the authors of the bible knew there were no ghosts in the machines.[2]

The Early Creeds

The New Testament, however, does express a belief in a life after death for human beings: the resurrection of Christ is a promise and guarantee of our own resurrection from the dead and eternal life with God. This faith in accord with sacred scripture was repeated in early Christian writings, particular in the ancient creeds. But also in accord with sacred scripture, belief was not expressed in the immortality of the soul, as if the soul could somehow survive the death of the body. Rather belief was expressed in "the resurrection of the dead" or "the resurrection of the body".

What this means we will have to discuss in some detail later. But for the moment notice only this: the ancient creeds proclaimed only that the whole physical human being by the power of God somehow survives after death. But the ancient creeds did not even suggest that the soul is immaterial, separate, and in itself immortal or that it can ever exist without the human body.

The canon of the New Testament, the "rule of faith," was nearly complete by about 200 a. d., thanks to the vigilance of episcopal authorities, but was not officially established until the third century, when the canon was declared by Pope Damasus and confirmed at the Council of Hippo in 393. It was not until then that ecclesiastical authorities finally identified specifically and officially which writings, among the many that were in circulation, counted as authentic testimony of the Christian faith.

But it was important from the earliest times that the genuine teaching of the apostles themselves be available to Christians in written form. The answer to this need was written creeds in the East and the West.

These were brief summaries of the "deposit of faith", the essential beliefs of a Christian. They were an effort, generally successful, to provide for Christians all over the world a touchstone of doctrinal unity and a criterion of apostolic continuity. It has been said that if the New Testament had not been written or preserved, we would be able to outline the distinctive Christian faith from the ancient creeds alone.

The creeds were not only a useful norm for genuine apostolic teaching. They were a conservative force as well, a checkpoint or watchdog against human innovations. To take an example that is of particular interest in this essay, after Platonic theologians introduced the Greek idea of the spirituality or immateriality of the human soul, the creeds kept teaching the biblical doctrine of the resurrection of the body.

Today, at least in the Catholic church, also in many other Christian churches, before baptism the catechumen recites the "Apostles' Creed". In the case of an infant the parents and godparents recite this creed in the name of the infant, and before first communion the children are required to memorize the Apostles' Creed and recite it themselves. And at every Sunday Mass Catholics in the East and the West recite the "Nicean Creed".

The oldest extant Greek text of the Apostles' Creed in original form is found in a letter from Marcellus of Ancyra to Pope Julius I written around 340 a. d. The oldest text in Latin is provided by Rufinus in *Commentary on the Symbol of the Apostles* around 400 a. d.

Rufinus claimed that this creed not only accurately reflected the teaching of the Apostles but that it was actually composed by them. He reported a tradition that after Pentecost the apostles "assembled in one spot and, being filled with the Holy Spirit, drafted this short summary of their future preaching, so that they might not find themselves, widely dispersed as they would be, delivering different messages."

It is more likely that the Apostles' Creed was first composed in Rome in a very brief and simple form at the beginning of the second century as a formula to be used in the liturgy of baptism. Gradually additions were made by different churches, and it was commonly accepted in its developed form in the West and the East at least by the time of the ecumenical Council of Nicea convoked by the emperor Constantine in 325, at which the Nicene Creed was formulated.

As mentioned above, both creeds profess faith in "the resurrection of the dead" or "of the body", not in "the immortality of the soul". The exact words used in these creeds were *carnis resurrectio* (resurrection of the flesh) in the West and ἀνάστᾶσις νεκρῶν (raising of the dead) in the East. The same is true of all the other professions of faith composed in the early church.

And even after Platonism and later Cartesianism infected parts of Christian theology, the creeds used in official liturgical celebrations today remain exactly the same. Christians still profess their belief in the resurrection of the dead, not in the immortality of the soul. For this expression of faith reflects more accurately the belief found in the New Testament rather than in some dualistic philosophy.

Chapter Four

Plato, Plotinus and Ancient Christian Writers

Early Ecclesiastical Writers

In addition to the Apostles' Creed, from the end of the first century to the beginning of the second we have copies of writings by Christians called "Apostolic Fathers". They got this name because of the early date of the text and because they themselves claimed to have been disciples of either some of the Apostles or of their immediate disciples. In any event, their teaching was in fact simply a continuation of apostolic preaching.

Some of these writings are epistles (Clement, Ignatius, Polycarp, Pseudo-Barnabus), and some are liturgical, parenetic or disciplinary treatises (The Didache, The Shepherd of Hermas, Homily of Clement, Papias).[1] The "Apostolic Fathers" made no attempt to speculate or philosophize about the teaching of the Apostles, only to repeat it. Christian theology and Christian philosophy did not begin until the time of the Greek apologists.

Historians sometimes speak of "the Platonism of the Fathers", and it is obvious that Plato, at least through Plotinus, deeply influenced the theological thinking of patristic writers. But we also find a good share of antiplatonism in ecclesiastical writers between the second and ninth centuries.

Dean William Inge in his *Philosophy of Plotinus* says, "Platonism is part of the vital structure of Christian theology, with which no other philosophy, I venture to say, can work without friction. There

is an utter impossibility of excising Platonism from Christianity
without tearing Christianity to pieces."[2] Although I believe that
this is an exaggeration, it is true that the neoplatonism of Plotinus
deeply influenced many Christian writers in the second and third
centuries, a time when Christianity was beginning to formulate
Christian doctrines for the first time in a theoretical and systematic
way.

Plato was born more than four hundred years before Christ,
and during his lifetime he created a genuine, complete and subtle
philosophy. His influence on the formulation of Christian doctrine
was through his writings and disciples but especially and princi-
pally through the neoplatonist, Plotinus.

At the Academy in Athens Plato's teachings were defended as
dogmas by his disciples until the middle of the second century before Christ, when changes occurred and a kind of neoplatonism
began to emerge. The greatest of these neoplatonists was Plotinus,
who lived in Alexandria between 204 and 270 a. d. Bertrand Russell
describes Plotinus as "the last of the great philosophers of antiquity"[3]

Plotinus emphasized the religious elements in Plato's thought,
so much so that one sometimes is inclined to think of him as teaching a religion rather than being a philosopher. In any event, the
philosophy of Plato and neoplatonism, especially the neoplatonism
of Plotinus, were useful to the Christian apologists who were working
in Greece in the second and third centuries.

According to Plato the mortal body is material and comes from
earth; the immortal soul is spiritual and comes from heaven. In
Phaedo before he drinks the hemlock Socrates explains that death
is the separation and release of the soul from the body. "And true
philosophers, and they alone," he says, "are ever seeking to release the soul." According to Plotinus, the Platonic form of the
Good is a kind of person, the Supreme Mind. From the Divine
Mind's contemplation of self emanates created beings, first Spirit,
the highest form of Being, from which emanates Soul, which in
turn ensouls matter. Matter is the lowest emanation, but like spirit
and soul it too is spiritual. The final goal of the soul is a kind of
mystical union with the God ("the One").

In the second century Christians could not be unaware of the pagan philosophies and wisdom of their time. So they wrote "apologies", intellectual and reasoned explanations of what they believed as Christians. They addressed these writings to pagans, but in fact they were meant for already believing Christians to explain to them that Christianity too offered a sound, reasonable philosophy and way of life, one that is true and in fact superior to that of pagans and Jews.

Earliest Apologists

Justin Martyr was born a pagan, sought meaning and understanding from four Greek philosophers, a Stoic, Peripatetic, Pythagorean and finally a Platonist. For a short time the Platonist satisfied him, until he met an old Christian who convinced him that the soul is not immortal in its own right, that the soul receives life from God and lives life only at God's pleasure, and lastly that Plato's doctrine of the transmigration of souls was mistaken.

Around 132 Justin converted to Christianity, and in his *Dialogue with Trypho*[4] he began to formulate his own theories about man. The soul of man, he thought, is created and corruptible. It has life only by the power and will of God. The body too is created and corruptible, and when the body dies man ceases to exist; but the soul leaves the body and continues to live unless and until God wills it to cease to be. So here with Justin we see the dualism of Plato start to have an effect on Christian thought about the nature of man.

Tatian, born in Syria around 120, converted to Christianity for a while but did not persevere in the faith. He studied under Justin in Rome, but unlike his master who loved and admired the Greeks, Tatian hated them, their philosophy, and culture.[5]

Tatian argued that according to the bible the soul is material because it exists in all things, but there is an immaterial spirit which is above it. If the soul does not know the truth, he says, it will die together with the body but will rise with the body so that it can share eternal punishment with it. Tatian is commonly described by historians as angry, severe and pessimistic. We need not try to make his doctrine more clear or precise than it probably was in his own mind.

Athenagorus, a coeval of Justin and Tatian, is distinguished for his apologia *On the Resurrection of the Dead*.[6] In his argument Athenagorus says that God did not create souls. He created men. Reason and understanding exist not in the soul but in man. Body and soul are one thing. They have one and the same generation, nature, life, actions and passions, and end. Athenagorus admired Greek philosophy, but his understanding of man was his own. It was not the dualism of the Greeks.

Irenaeus was born in Asia Minor around 126 and was priest and bishop of Lyons after 177 until he died sometime between 193 and 211. He campaigned against developing heresies, especially Gnosticism and Montanism in the early days of Christianity. Irenaeus was familiar with and in some areas of his theology indebted to Plato. In fact he once said that Plato had seen the truth better than the Gnostics.

Nonetheless, Irenaeus at bottom was leery of any philosophic approach to Christianity, because it had infected many of the heretical doctrines that he was fighting against. Irenaeus believed that Christianity rested on revelation, tradition and the power of the Holy Spirit. The source and foundation of Christian theology, he thought, was the bible not philosophical speculations.[7]

For Irenaeus *spirit* is clearly identified as a religious notion. It is the supernatural element that is not part of human nature but given to it by the Holy Spirit. Souls are natural to man but do not transmigrate from body to body. The body is the soul's instrument, but the soul itself is wholly material.

In comparison to the body, however, the soul can be said to be incorporeal, for it is the breath of life breathed into man by God. Therefore as long as God wills it to live, the human soul does not die. After a man's death the soul goes to some invisible place, where it waits for the resurrection of the body.

Therefore for Irenaeus the soul of man is material but for a short time can be separated from the body. This explanation, obviously is not Platonism but a theory of Irenaeus' own making, reflecting both the New Testament and Greek philosophy.

The Beginning of Systematic Christian Theology

The end of the second century was occupied with a variety of religious beliefs—ancient paganism, neo-pythagorianism, a Persian religion called Mithraism, Gnosticism, and Christianity; and Alexandria for a long time had been and still was a focal spot for the religions of the Roman Empire.

The number of Christians had increased largely through a process of natural growth. But at the start of the third century a new confidence and missionary spirit developed, and Christians began serious efforts to convert educated pagans to Christianity first in Alexandria, then in Carthage and Rome. The principals in this endeavor were Clement of Alexandria, Origen, Tertullian, Gregory Nazianzenus, Basil the Great, and Gregory of Nyssa. In the pages that follow we will concentrate only on their anthropology, which was only a minor part of their grand syntheses.

Clement, a convert to Christianity, settled in Alexandria. He held that while philosophy was necessary for the Greek, it was not for the Christian, who needs only the doctrine of Christ for salvation. However, he acknowledged, philosophy can be useful to a Christian, as long as it is kept in its proper place, the place of the "handmaiden" to Christian thought. But philosophy, he said, can help in leading men to faith and to understand it after it is received. Nonetheless it is generally agreed by historians that the philosophy of the Greeks played a very important role in Clement's formulation of his Christian theology.[8]

Clement taught that human souls did not preexist but that they are immortal. But what exactly Clement thought about the nature of the human soul is not clear and has different interpretations. He only said that the human soul is more simple and more subtle than water, and at least in this sense it can be said to be incorporeal. And all souls, of animals and men, are invisible.

Origen was born of Christian parents in 185, taught in Alexandria between 202 and 215, then in Palestine for the next fifteen years. Escaping martyrdom, he died in Tyre when he was 69 years old. Unlike Clement there is no ambiguity in Origen about his commitment to Greek philosophy, specifically to neoplatonism as impressed on him by another Christian named Ammonius Saccus, at whose school Origen may have met Plotinus.

No one up to this time was as learned in both the bible and in philosophy as Origen, and he created for the first time a philosophical structure into which the Christian view of the world could be integrated. The creation was magnificent, though not without errors.[9]

As to his anthropology, Origen adopted Ammonius' understanding of the world as populated by spiritual substances, each of which was put in charge of his own body. Thanks to the prestige and influence of Origen this neoplatonic theory came in to common use by Christian writers especially in the East.

Origen believed in the resurrection of the dead and that rational souls will be eternally punished or rewarded according to their free decisions. But he also noted that the literal interpretation of this teaching, that the same physical body that dies gets up out of the grave, is the doctrine as it is preached in the churches for the simple-minded and the common crowds, so that they will be motivated to live better lives. But it is only an allegory for the more exact doctrine that after death a new body rises, a body that is appropriate to the new and immortal life.

Origen was so interested in the resurrection of the dead that he wrote two treatises on the topic. He speculates on the nature of the rational soul, whether it is corporeal or incorporeal. The word ἀσώματον (incorporeal), he says, does not appear in the New Testament. Besides, he notes, Justin, Tatian, Athenagorus, Irenaeus and others did not think that the materiality of souls was incompatible with the Christian faith. But Origen himself preferred Greek philosophy on this matter.

Tertullian, one of the most famous Latin writers, was born at Carthage around 160, and converted to Christianity sometime between 190 and 195. He became a Montanist for a short time (c. 206-13), then rejected Montanism and kept writing his theology. He died about the year 240.

Tertullian was a fierce enemy of philosophy. As St. Peter warned in his second epistle, he said, philosophy is the wisdom of the world and it fosters heresies. He also quotes St. Paul, who had visited Athens: "Take care that nobody exploits you through the pretensions of philosophy, guided by human tradition, . . . instead of following Christ."[10] Tertullian asked rhetorically: "What has Athens to do with Jerusalem? What has the Academy to do with the Church?" The rule of faith, he said, was entrusted by Christ, not to philosophers, but to the Apostles and the Church. For Tertullian the function of human reason was to understand the Scriptures and divine revelation contained therein.[11]

Tertullian's *De Anima* is his second longest treatise. Here he asks three questions about the human soul: 1) What is the soul? 2) What is its origin? and 3) What happens to it after death? Tertullian is clear and adamant about the nature of the soul. The human soul is composed of one thing, and that thing is matter. Man is body and soul, and the soul is also a body. The soul is more fluid and subtle than the external body whose form it takes. But both are material.[12] The soul is simple. If it is called "spirit" it is only because it "respires" or breathes, not because it is not a body.

As to its origin, the soul is created by God, transmitted to the baby as a fragment of the father's soul, and as a result the image of God and original sin are passed down from generation to generation. This, of course, Tertullian warned, has nothing to do with the Greek idea of transmigration, which is an absurd doctrine. Finally after death all souls, except the souls of martyrs, descend into hell to await the resurrection of the body and the final judgment.

Arnobius was born around 260 and converted to Christianity sometime between 296 and 307. The only thing useful to note is that he was another fervent anti-Platonist. Men are not souls, he said. They are rational but rarely use their reason. Contrary to Plato he argued that souls are corporeal and some of them in fact will die and be annihilated.[13]

Lactantius was born in Africa at an unknown date. He was a convert to Christianity, according to St. Jerome. He was a student of Arnobius and was critical of all pagan philosophy, Latin and Greek. Unlike Christianity which unites religion and wisdom, paganism separates them. As a result the pagans accept false religion and false wisdom. In his *De opificio Dei*[14] he explains that since the soul cannot be seen, it cannot be defined. It is in the whole body and is nourished by the blood, as light is nourished by oil. Philosophers, he said, have never agreed about the nature of the soul, and they never will.

Gregory of Nyssa was made a bishop by his older brother St. Basil in 371. His philosophy generally followed neoplatonism, and he was an admirer of Origen. He wrote *De Hominis opificio*[15] in which he outlined his understanding of man. Man has a place in the physical world by his body and in the invisible world by his soul. But Plato was wrong in thinking that the soul preexisted the body.

The most difficult question concerns the manner in which the soul and the body are united. Gregory doubts that the answer to this question will ever be fully understood, because the soul in the last analysis is incomprehensible. The soul is incorporeal and therefore cannot be contained in a particular place. It has a body as an instrument in order to think and to speak. And even between death and resurrection the elements of the dead body are never completely separated from the soul.

Another work *De anima* was incorrectly attributed to Gregory but is in fact a work of Nemesius called *De natura hominis*.[16] Nemesius was a disciple of Greek philosophers, especially Plato and Plotinus. His work could easily be classified as belonging to the history of philosophy rather than theology.

St. Augustine (354-430) was born at Thagaste in North Africa about sixty miles inland from the Mediterranean Sea. He studied at Carthage (370), embraced Manicheism (315-376), finally rejected Manicheism (382), went to Rome (383), listened to sermons of St. Ambrose in Milan, read some neoplatonic writings including some *Enneads* of Plotinus, read the writings of St. Paul, was encouraged by the conversion of the famous Platonist Marius Victorinus, accepted Christianity himself and was baptized by St. Ambrose in 387. He returned to his birthplace in Hippo, was ordained a priest and in 395 or 396 became bishop of Hippo, where he spent the rest of his life. He was probably the most influential writer in Christianity since St. Paul.

Based on his early writings it has been said that "morally as well as intellectually [Augustine] was converted to Neoplatonism rather than to the gospel."[17] But the truth is that in 386 Augustine accepted the gospel not only without any reservation, but in opposition to the neoplatonist Porphyry, who had previously been of great help to him.[18] Augustine had altogether renounced Manicheism, but occasionally there are traces of it in some of his writings. Augustine frequently looked to neoplatonism for help in solving some problems, and in that sense he can be described as philosophically a neoplatonist. But he was more concerned with limiting the invasion of neoplatonism into Christian theology than introducing it.[19]

St. Augustine was the most voluminous writer among the Western Fathers. But most of his writings and the most important ones were in Dogmatic Theology (e.g. 15 books *De Trinitate*) and a systematic explanation of Christian doctrine called *Enchiridion ad Laurentium*. Apologetics (e.g. *Civitate Dei*, the most widely read book after his *Confessions)*, Exegesis (e.g. *De Doctrina Christiana)*, and Polemical writings (e.g. *De Haeresibus* and *De Gratia et Libero Arbitrio)*, plus many homilies and books on Christian morality.

But he did write down some of his ideas on anthropology, for instance *De anima et eius Origine Libri Quatuor*, which deals with the immortality of the soul;[20] and two dialogues *De Quantitate Animae* written to prove the immateriality of the soul.[21] Here he used the philosophy of neoplatonism, which he said was best suited to bring people to Christian faith.[22]

Augustine never thought that man is a soul apart from its body or a body apart from the soul. But like Plato he defined man as a soul using its body. For Augustine this did not quite mean that man is essentially a soul but that the soul has a transcendental superiority over the body. Here the anthropology of Plotinus is apparent.

Since the soul is incorporeal and the body which the soul uses is corporeal, Augustine was puzzled about the way they are united. He never quite resolved this problem. He only explained that the soul is life itself and therefore is the life of the body. The body gets its life from the soul. When it dies it disintegrates. But the soul lives on, since it is by its very nature a living substance.

With this, although he does not resolve the fundamental problem created by his dualism, he achieves his own polemic purpose which is to defend the immortality of the human soul. In fact, he seems to emphasize the immortality of the spiritual soul over the resurrection of the material body.

Although Augustine here obviously explained Christian doctrine in terms of Plato's philosophy, his teaching cannot simply be reduced to that of Plato or Plotinus. The Greeks and Augustine operated out of quite different principles and had quite different objectives. Etienne Gilson pointed out that the Christian writers of this time were opportunists.

They used Greek philosophy when it seemed helpful to their own purposes. But they rejected it when it did not, for instance Plato's doctrine "that matter is eternal, that God is a mere demiurge not a true creator, that ideas are eternal entities subsisting in themselves apart from God, that human souls are immortal by nature, that souls pre-exist bodies, that there is a transmigration of soul from body to body", and so on.[23]

We might mention one thing more. In St. Augustine's mind man is a unique combination of spirit, which is next to God (*prope Deum*) and matter, which is next to nothing (*prope nihil*). But he did use the term *spiritual matter* (as did some of his later disciples).[24]

What exactly he means by this term is not clear. St. Augustine used the words *spirit* and *spiritual* with a great variety of meanings. But he never simply reduced spirit to matter or soul to body. However in a rather strange epistemology Augustine used the word *spirit* to designate an "imaginative faculty" which is something less than the whole soul and less spiritual than the intellect, which is the soul's highest and most spiritual faculty. The imaginative faculty represents corporeal objects to the intellect. It is an intermediate faculty bridging the gap between the intellect and matter and called by Augustine "spirit". Spirit in this sense is not body in itself, but it is inferior to the intellect, which is totally independent of matter.[25]

After Augustine ecclesiastical writers like Denis the Areopagite (535-570) and Maximus the Confessor (580-667) kept the neoplatonic anthropology alive in the East. But theologians in the West did not go in the same direction. An Irishman, John Scotus Erigina (810-877),[26] carried on the tradition of Augustine in the West, but his example was not followed by others. Western Europe was being tempted to a different kind of metaphysics.

Manlius Sererinus Boethius was born about 480 and went to Athens to study philosophy, where he was impressed by the thinking of Aristotle. He decided to translate into Latin all the writings of Plato and Aristotle. But in this endeavor he did not get very far, and what he did get done was somewhat shabby. Nonetheless Boethius' own anthropology sounds more Aristotelian than Platonic.

Man, Boethius says, is not a soul, nor is he a body. He is a composite of body and soul—that is, matter organized as a body and a soul which organizes the matter into a body. The soul is not what (*quod*) a man is; it is that by which (*quo*) he is what he is. In other words, the soul is not the substance that is man but only the form which determines the substance to be what it is.[27]

A better understating of Aristotle in the West had to await a better translation of his writings, which happened around 840, first into Arabic by the Christian Arab, Ibn Abdallah Naima, and later into Latin by the Dominican William of Moerbeke.

At Chartres in the beginning of the twelfth century a new "Platonist movement" developed. But the teaching of Plato in circulation there was second hand, and there were many versions of it. It is not true to say that the only thing ever discussed there was the problem of the universal. But one story tells of a student who left there for three years, and when he returned he found the same people involved in the very same discussion that they were engaged in when he left. Boethius had left them two solutions to the problem, one from Plato and the other from Aristotle. But since both systems were unknown, little progress was made.

It is no surprise that in the 11th century St. Peter Damian (1007-72) said that if philosophy were necessary to save mankind, God would have sent philosophers to convert it, not fishermen.

Summary of Patristic Doctrine

Unlike the canonical scriptures and the ancient creeds, early Christian writers were divided on the nature of the human soul.

Some, enamored of Greek philosophy, attempted to explain Christian doctrine in categories of Plato and neoplatonists like Plotinus as far as they could without accepting any of Greek philosophy which would contradict the Christian faith. Thus Origen, Gregory of Nyssa, and Augustine taught that man is composed of a material body and a spiritual soul which uses the body as its instrument in this life and survives it after death.

Others were leery of Greek philosophy for fear that it might lead them away from the teaching of God as it is contained in the bible. These were Tatian, Athenagorus, Irenaeus, Tertullian, and Arnobius. Some who held that the human soul is made of matter like the body also admitted the possibility of the soul's separation from the body after death, while it awaits the final resurrection of the body.

Finally, the views of Justin, Lactantius and St. Clement about the soul are not clear and can be interpreted differently.

Chapter Five

Aristotle, Medieval Scholasticism and Thomas Aquinas

Five centuries before Christ Greek physics held that everything was made out of four elements—earth, water, fire, and spirit—and that the smallest unit of things was an atom. Democritus, of course, did not use the word *atom* in its modern scientific sense. He used it in its etymological sense, meaning (tautologically) something indivisible, a thing that cannot be split into a smaller thing. Aristotle also wrote a book on physics. It was not entirely aprioristic, was based on observation, but was hardly experimental or a scientific breakthrough.

But he did write another book in which he created a metaphysics that was a breakthrough or at least a systematic philosophy that has had a wide and profound influence down through history and in a few places is still cultivated today. Aristotle explained all reality or being in categories of act and potency, form and matter, substance and nine accidents.

Translations of some of the writings of Aristotle into Latin began with Boethius as early as the sixth century. Gradually Latin translations of the writings of Aristotle, mixed indiscriminately with writings of Plato, neoplatonists and Arabian philosophers, began to appear and be read in the West. Successful translations into Latin directly from the Greek were finally made at the beginning of the thirteenth century by William of Moerbeke (1215-1236) and others around the time that the University of Paris was being established (c. 1215).

From the very beginning translations of the scientific treatises of Aristotle and his Arabian commentators appeared *in the classrooms* of the masters in the Faculty of Arts. The immediate consequence was the prohibition of their use by ecclesiastical authorities. The prohibition, of course, led to a sudden increase of interest in Aristotle. From then on Plato was studied by day, and Aristotle was read at night.

The masters in the Faculty of Theology found neoplatonism easier to reconcile with St. Augustine, and so they were more restrained in their public use of Aristotle, especially since Aristotle had been interdicted by Pope Gregory IX in 1228 and 1231. But they continued to study the ideas of Aristotle in their efforts to more adequately explain Christian theology. After 1250 warnings against Aristotle continued to be issued by ecclesiastical authorities, but prohibitions were discontinued, and by 1366 Aristotle was required reading in the Faculty of Arts.

Scholastic theologians differed on and debated many doctrinal issues. But they generally agreed that the human soul is a spiritual substance. However, since man is one being, they had to explain how the spiritual soul was related to the material body. To this question the masters before St. Thomas Aquinas stammered a variety of responses. But none of them was willing to say that the soul is the form of the body as Aristotle said.

To apply Aristotle's doctrine of hylomorphism to explain the union of a material body and a spiritual soul, they believed, would compromise the Christian doctrine of immortality. They chose a solution reminiscent of the definition of man given by Plato, Plotinus and St. Augustine, that is a spiritual soul who uses a body, in other words "a ghost in a machine."

St. Augustine was a great if not the best theologian in the Christian past. The common respect and admiration for St. Augustine at the time was reinforced by Gregory IX who instructed the faculty at the University of Paris to always remain faithful to the teachings of St. Augustine.

In this context St. Thomas Aquinas said for the first time exactly what Aristotle had said—that the soul is the form of the body.

This is to say that spirit is the form of matter, and together they form one unified being which is man.

According the Aristotle's hylomorphism, the form of matter is its actualization, i.e. what brings it into being. What is more, neither matter nor form can exist without the other. Prime matter of itself is nothing; in itself it is mere potency for being and cannot exist without a form. And form is act; it is the actualization of prime matter and has no being except in so far as it is fulfilling its proper function, which is to actualize matter.

Accordingly, it is easy to see why other scholastic theologians were unwilling simply to adopt hylomorphism as a Christian solution to the body/soul problem in the thirteenth century.

St. Thomas was not a philosopher searching for pure philosophical truth. He was a monk and a Christian theologian trying to use the most reasonable philosophical wisdom to explain and clarify the Christian faith. So to accomplish his end he simply changed the metaphysics of Aristotle to accommodate the theology of St. Augustine.

If the spiritual soul is the form of a material body, Thomas would be asked, why does it not perish with the body, since man is an organic whole, that is one unified being? It is no surprise that unlike Plato Aristotle did not defend the immortality of souls. For according to hylomorphism matter cannot exist without form, and form cannot exist without matter. Once St. Thomas rejected Plato's philosophical idea that the relation between the soul and the body is merely an accidental one, that the soul is a spiritual substance using a material body, he ran into a more important theological problem.

To solve this problem St. Thomas used Aristotelian categories even though he radically departed from Aristotelian metaphysics. He explained that the spiritual form is itself actualized by *esse* (existence) and so it is able to continue to be after the death of the body. Thomas accepted Aristotle's hylomorphism until he thought it became incompatible with religious dogma. See, for instance, Quodlibet *Tertium,* where, Thomas asked: Can God make it possible for matter to exist without form? and answered that this is a contradiction in terms, which even God cannot make happen.[1]

St. Thomas was a follower of St. Augustine but he did not accept his Platonism. He was also a follower of Aristotle, but in this very complicated body/soul issue he was not altogether faithful to Aristotle either.

St. Thomas' opinion was that even the power of God cannot make matter exist without a form, since matter without a form is a contradiction in terms. But then what about a form? Is it not a contradiction in terms for a form to have existence without actuating or informing matter?

In his *Quaestio Disputata De Anima*[2] St. Thomas inquired: Is it possible for the human soul to be a form and a singular thing (*et hoc aliquid*)? Thomas first reports a strong argument for a negative response to this question: If the human soul is in itself a singular or individuated thing it is in itself subsistent, i.e. in itself a complete being, and therefore according to Aristotle it cannot be the form of another being but only accidentally united to it.

Thomas responds that even if the soul has complete being, it does not necessarily follow that it is only accidentally united to the body. For the soul communicates its own existence (*esse*) to the body, so that there is only one *esse* of the unified composite. Besides, he adds, even though the human soul is in itself subsistent, in itself it does not have a complete species; the body completes its species.

According to Thomas the soul does not have merely an accidental relationship to its body. The soul does not merely use the body as an instrument. Rather it is the form of the body in the Aristotelian hylomorphic sense. Therefore the human body and soul form together one unified organic whole, one living rational thing. Nonetheless the soul can exist for a time after death while it awaits the resurrection of its body at the end of the world.

So for Thomas, unlike Augustine, there is no "ghost in the machine", at least while a man is alive. But at death somehow a "ghost" survives for a short time until it can be reunited to form again the same one unified whole with its body. Neoplatonism was now having less but still some influence on Christian thought.

The End of Medieval Scholasticism

A short time after St. Thomas died, at least by the beginning of the fourteenth century, medieval scholasticism began to decline, disintegrate, and decay. At the beginning there were two principal reasons for this. One was attacks from outside by Averroism (a new Arabic interpretation of Aristotle) and Ochhamism (a systematic skepticism about the possibility of any certitude from philosophy or metaphysics).

The other was from inside and was more damaging. The metaphysics of Aristotle was no longer suspect. In fact, it had become the authoritative standard among the theologians of the day. Pope Clement VI even criticized some of the students at the University of Paris for neglecting the wisdom of Aristotle in so far as it did not contradict the faith. What is more, a few years later popes required that the masters of Paris follow a system that was called "Aristotle not contrary to faith".

As a result Aristotle was so purified that neither Thomas, nor Averroes, nor Aristotle would have recognized it. "Aristotle not contrary to faith" was not able to support a rational theological system. It was finally replaced with the coming of new secular ideas about the nature of man during the Renaissance, Enlightenment and contemporary times.

Chapter Six

Authoritative Teaching and Prescribed Seminary Textbooks

What is the norm of faith for Christians? What is their source of God's revelation? What exactly do Christians base their beliefs on? For Orthodox, Protestant and Catholic Christians the answer is the same: the norm of Christian faith for all Christians is the Sacred Scriptures. Also, for most Christians today, the norm of faith is not what the words of the bible literally say but what they mean in the context and literary form in which they were written.

The bible contains different forms of literature, for example poetry, fiction, myths, parenesis, midrash, folklore, popular (nonscientific) history, etc. And how do readers of the bible know the difference? Sometimes the literary form will be obvious to them, and sometimes they will have to depend on the conclusions of biblical scholars.

From the beginning to get a clearer and more authentic understanding of the teachings in the bible a magisterium or teaching authority developed in the Catholic Church in both the East and the West. This magisterium consisted mainly of bishops in their own dioceses or gathered together in councils, and after a time the bishop of Rome acquired a kind of preeminent role in settling theological disputes.

After the Great Schism in the Eastern part of the Church, the Orthodox relied on the teaching of the first seven ecumenical councils and the teaching of their own bishops in the East. This system worked very well. Even today the Roman Catholic Church technically considers the Eastern or Orthodox Church as schismatic, not heretical. That is to say that the Orthodox Church has a different juridical and disciplinary structure but teaches the same faith as is taught in the Roman or Western part of the Church.

In the West in the thirteenth century the theological faculties in the new European universities gained some importance in settling theological disputes, but they never supplanted the bishops as the primary teachers or guarantors of the faith. In the sixteenth century Martin Luther and other Protestant Reformers introduced the idea of private interpretation of the bible. Individual Christians under the guidance of the Holy Spirit can interpret the meaning of the bible for themselves and often better than any external authority.

Luther's new idea about the way Christians learn God's revelation brought its own problems, for example unclarity about divine revelation, sectarianism, and a somewhat fuzzy definition of Christianity. But it also prevented many of the abuses that existed in the ancient Catholic system. Christians no longer were expected to accept heteronomously the thinking of others, and they would be free to investigate in a scholarly way new ideas without being prevented or stifled by non-scholarly ecclesiastical authorities simply because they are ecclesiastical authorities.

One of the effects of Luther's new idea was to bring about gradually a moderation and in some instances the elimination of some of the abuses in the Catholic magisterium. And while some of the problems inherent in the Lutheran policy of private interpretation did occur, doctrinal chaos did not ensue as was often predicted. It was held in check by scholarly academic debate, Christian tradition, pastoral preaching, and again by the ecclesiastical authorities that still existed in many denominations.

Hierarchy of Truths

There are some people who prefer certitude over truth. Their goal is always to be certain; for them knowing the truth is secondary. The normal person, on the other hand, knows that what is most important is the truth, even if it can be known only with probability.

Very often probable knowledge is all that is available in human affairs, and so also in religion. Some people think that it should be otherwise. They feel that we should be able to get certitude at least in religion. That probably is the reason some people are attracted to fundamentalism in any religion, even in Christianity. But mainstream Protestantism knows that certitude in theological questions is not easily available. So do the Catholic and Orthodox Churches.

Between 1962 and 1965, with Protestant and Orthodox observers, the Catholic bishops scattered throughout the world met together in Vatican City as the Second Vatican Council. This was the magisterium at work in the twentieth century at its highest level.

In their *Decree on Ecumenism* the bishops said:

Ecumenical action cannot but be fully and sincerely Catholic— faithful, that is, to the truth which we have received from the apostles and fathers, and in harmony with the faith which the Catholic Church has always confessed. But we should always preserve the sense of an order based on degree, of a 'hierarchy' in the truths of Catholic doctrine which, although they all demand a due assent of faith, do not all occupy the same principal or central place in the mystery revealed in Jesus Christ, since they vary in their relationship to the foundation of the Christian faith.

Students should learn to distinguish between revealed truths, which all require the same assent of faith, and theological doctrines. Hence they should be taught to distinguish between 'the deposit of faith itself, or the truths that are contained in our venerable doctrine,' and the way in which they are enunciated, between the truth to be enunciated and the various ways of perceiving and more clearly illustrating it, between apostolic tradition and merely ecclesiastical traditions. Already, from the time of their philosophical training, students should be put in a frame of mind to recognize that different ways of stating things in theology too are legitimate and reasonable, because of the diversity of methods or ways by which theologians understand and express divine revelation. Thus it is that these various theological formulae are often complementary rather than conflicting.[1]

This was not new. Theologians long ago had invented a system of "theological notes" to designate where a particular doctrine fit on the hierarchical scale of "truths". Some doctrines were designated "of divine faith" (i.e. revealed by God), some "of divine and catholic faith" (i.e. revealed by God and taught by all the bishops in the world), and some "of defined faith" (i.e. designated as divine revelation by the bishop of Rome in union with all the other bishops either dispersed throughout the world or more commonly assembled in an ecumenical council). These doctrines were considered certain and irreformable Catholic beliefs.

Because of disputes and arguments among theologians it is not always certain which doctrinal statements fit into one of these categories. Following the norm set up in the old code of canon law (1918) , the new code (1983) in canon 749 says that unless it is clearly and certainly established as such no doctrine is to be considered infallibly or absolutely irreformable.

There are a variety of other "theological notes" used by theologians, for example the teaching of "the ordinary magisterium" of the pope or bishops, a common theological opinion, a more probable opinion, and so on. These doctrines may be true, in fact they may at the moment be considered certain. But none of them are so certain that they cannot be changed in the future in the light of new and convincing evidence.[2]

These theological notes were used in the textbooks which were used to teach Catholic seminarians everywhere in the world between 1850 and 1950. These textbooks were written in Latin by professors in some of the most distinguished seminaries in the world.

They consisted of four, six, or more volumes and contained systematically on its thousands of pages a great number of theses, statements of Catholic doctrine, which were explained and then defended by augments from the bible, the early fathers of the Church, statements of ecumenical councils, and if possible human reason. Each thesis' proper place in "the hierarchy of truths" was indicated by its appropriate "theological note". If the correct theological note was disputed by theologians, the careful author usually indicated this in his text.

With this as background we can take a look at the way two prominent seminary textbooks talked about the human soul and how they interpreted official documents of the magisterial authority of the Church.

Seminary Textbooks (c. 1850–1960)

The two best manuals, widely used in Catholic seminaries from the middle of the nineteenth century to the middle of the twentieth, were Lercher's *Institutiones Theologiae Dogmaticae* from the University of Innsbruck[3] and Dalmau's and Sagues' *Sacrae Theologiae Summa* from the University of Salamanca.[4]

Lercher defends three theses that are of special interest here.

1. First, he asserts that "the human soul truly, per se and essentially is the form of the body." To this thesis he assigns the theological note "solemnly defined" (*solemniter definita*) at the Council of Vienne in 1311-1312[5] and at the Fifth Lateran Council in 1512-1517.[6]

The exact meaning of this thesis, he explains, is that the human soul is an essential constituent of human nature; that is, it is not united accidentally to the body and cannot exist outside the body without the body ceasing to be a human body. For with the body the soul forms one nature, one substance.[7] Sagues says the same thing, adding only that in *Eximian tuam*[8] written to the Archbishop of Cologne Pope Pius IX condemned the dualistic anthropology of A. Gunther, saying that the teaching of St. Thomas Aquinas on this matter is to be held by all.[9]

2. Second, Lercher asserts that "the human soul is immortal". That the human soul is de facto immortal, he says, has been defined as a dogma in 1512-1517 at the Fifth Lateran Council.[10] That the soul is naturally immortal is almost a matter of faith (*proxima fidei*). Sagues repeats the same doctrine and arguments but with more detail.[11]

3. The third related thesis in Lercher is that the human soul is spiritual. The word *spirit* as used here, Lercher explains, does not designate a pure spirit, which is absolutely independent of all mat-

ter. Rather it designates a spiritual substance, "a substance which is not matter, nor a constitutive part of matter, nor intrinsically dependent on matter in being or operation" (in *esse et operari*); it only is dependent on matter "extrinsically".

This means that while the human soul is the essential form of matter, in itself it does not depend on matter as an accident which inheres in a substance or as a material form in irrational animals or plants.

As to the ecclesiastical authority supporting his thesis, Lercher admits that all relevant conciliar definitions do not speak of the spirituality of the soul directly but only incidentally and indirectly (*obiter et indirecte*). So the doctrine of the spirituality of the soul was never the direct object of any conciliar teaching.

However, he says, the thesis is "of divine and catholic faith", that is, revealed by God and taught as such by the bishops throughout the world. Therefore, he concludes, this doctrine must belong to the "deposit of faith", that is the faith left to us by Christ and the Apostles. Besides, he says, the spirituality of the soul can be proved with certitude by natural human reason.

That the spirituality of human souls can be proved by human reason is certainly doubtful. So is his opinion that this doctrine is (1) divinely revealed and (2) taught as such by the universal Church. As evidence that the human soul is spiritual in the sense he describes in the explanation of the term that he gives above, Lercher points to several texts in the bible where the soul is called "spirit" and contra distinguished from the body. Consider for instance, *Ooheleth* (*Ecclesiastes*) 12, 7: "And the dust returns to the earth as it was. And the spirit returns to God who gave it."

However, contemporary biblical scholarship interprets this text quite differently. *The Jerome Biblical Commentary* reads *pneuma* as "life breath" and says, "Death is described in terms of Gen. 2:7; the breath returns to God. This is not the soul, and there is no statement of immortality here (cf. 9:10). In 3:21 he questioned whether there was any difference between the breath in humans and animals. Here he is simply affirming that God is the author of that breath."[12]

Another argument is made from Mt. 10, 28: "Have no fear of those who kill the body but cannot kill the soul. You had better be afraid of one who can destroy both soul and body in the pit". But, as we noted above in our analysis of the use of *psyche* in the New Testament, it frequently designates not natural life but the new supernatural life of the Christian.

Commenting on the same text McKenzie simply says, "The life lost here is evidently not the natural life, for the *psyche* dies; it is the new life of the Christian."[13]

As evidence for the second part of his theological note Lercher observes that in catechisms, public preaching, and religious books the human soul is described as similar to angels. This argument has some verisimilitude. At least it is a sign that the spirituality of the soul, although never formally defined in an ecumenical council, is universally taught in the Catholic Church.

But that is not enough. To be counted as a dogma a doctrine must be universally taught as such, that is as a divinely revealed truth, by Catholic bishops dispersed throughout the world. But that there is such a consensus about the nature of the human soul is far from clear. Even the early Church Fathers were not in agreement about the soul's spirituality. In fact, as we have seen, many explicitly denied it precisely because they believed that it was not contained in divine revelation.

In his seminary manual Sagues does not even have a thesis on the spirituality of the soul. He only has a seven paragraph note called a "scholion" on the topic. He repeats the same doctrine of Lercher but more economically.

In a footnote he quotes another contemporary theologian who explained that the bible and church documents were more occupied with the immortality of the soul than its spirituality, because the former is what really interests people. As a result the spirituality of the soul has been taught in church documents only obliquely or implicitly.[14]

Summary

It is a dogma of the Catholic faith that there is no "ghost in the machine". This may come as surprise after the confusion created by St. Augustine and Origen in the third century, at a time when Christian doctrine was being formulated for the first time in a thematic and systematic way. But when the smoke cleared the Church in its official teaching held fast to the doctrine of the New Testament and the ancient creeds. It rejected dualism of every kind, Platonic, Augustinian, Cartesian, and committed itself irretrievably to anthropological monism. Man is one substance, one person, one thing. Her body and soul form essentially one and the same being called man.

The Catholic Church has committed itself in the same way to the teaching of the New Testament and the ancient creeds that man, by a free gift from God, is immortal and will live forever. But it has not taught more than this. It has not officially taught that human immortality can be proven by reason alone or that immortality is natural to man because she has an immaterial soul.

The spirituality of the human soul is not necessary to defend or make possible the immortality of man. In the past it seemed to some apologists that the doctrine of human immortality would be easier to explain and defend if one included Plato's idea of a spiritual soul. But to make this doctrine depend on Plato's idea of a spiritual soul probably makes it more incredible. Nothing can make this mystery of God's gratuitous love for man easy to explain, and a claim that natural human reason can prove that an immaterial spirit exists within man makes the doctrine even more difficult to believe.

In fact, that the human soul is immaterial and thus radically different from the material body is not clear in church documents. To assert the spirituality of the soul would represent a serious qualification of the Church's defined dogma, a qualification found not in the New Testament or ancient creeds but only in pagan philosophy.

It is not surprising, therefore, that the spirituality of the human soul never has been formally or expressly taught in Church documents. It is only assumed in the language chosen to express its dogmatic teaching. But to assume is not the same as to teach. At most it is taught in church documents only *"implicite"*, *"indirecte"* and *"obiter."*

It seems at least probable, therefore, that in the Church's dogmatic pronouncements man is, á la Madonna, a wholly material girl.

Chapter Seven

Contemporary Christian Theology

John Hick

In a first class book entitled *Death and Eternal Life*[1] Protestant theologian John Hick (Fellow of the Institute for Advanced Research in the Humanities at the University of Birmingham in England) details the thinking about life after death of several important Protestant theologians of our time—Oscar Cullman, Paul Tillich, Charles Hartshorne, and Wolfhart Pannenberg.

One issue in Protestant theology, he says, is whether the human soul is of its very nature immortal and lives on forever independently of any further decision of God, or is man naturally mortal and can be raised from the dead only by a special act of God. In an influential lecture, *Immortality of the Soul or Resurrection of the Dead,* Oscar Cullman argues that the answer to this question is not of primary importance. For in either case unending life is a free gift of the Creator to his creature.

Nevertheless, Hick points out, there is another question hiding in this question: Is there an implied distinction here between an embodied and disembodied existence after death and if so what does either type of existence entail? Cullman does not consider this question, which eventually should be asked.

Hick then describes Paul Tillich's understanding of eternal life as a participation in eternity by being remembered by God. Hick says that Tillich employs the "bold metaphor" of man's immortality within the eternal divine memory. This eternal divine memory retains only the good and eliminates the bad, since in itself evil is nothing.

But what does this mean, Hick asks, as regards human existence or non-existence after death? Hick finds Tillich's response at least confusing and more likely self-contradictory. For Tillich "rejects the notion of the continued life of an individual beyond the grave . . . But only a little later Tillich asserts that the 'self-conscious self cannot be denied to the biological dimension and therefore to the body.'"

Charles Hartshorne, Hick says, also believes that human immortality means that after our death we and our lives will be remembered forever by God. So we will live on in the complete and infallible memory of God." This is certainly clearer and less confusing than Tillich's explanation, but it is not a description of life after death in any real sense, at least not in the accustomed sense. What continues to live after an individual person's death is not that person but only God's memory of him.

Finally Hick describes the theory of Wolfhart Pannenberg as expressed in 1968 in the third edition of his *What is Man? Present-day Anthropology in the Light of Theology*. In Pannenberg's theory we speak in metaphor of "the immortality of the soul" and of "the resurrection of the body". But if the first implies that "a part of man" [the soul or the mind] continues beyond death in an unbroken way it makes no real sense. For the mind or consciousness is so intertwined with our bodily functions that a separation of mind or soul from the body is impossible. Accordingly, there can be no human consciousness after the physical death of the human body.

So Pannenberg chooses the other metaphor, "resurrection of the body". Pannenberg says that this occurs neither before nor after death; presumably therefore it occurs at the very instant of death, when man as a whole is transferred out of time into the eternity of the timeless state of God. At this point nothing is changed about man's life except his new existence in an ever-present now. Otherwise it stays the same as it was when he lived in time. Also if he has not had a saving encounter with Jesus during his life so as to have a right relationship with God, he will exist under judgment, always aware of his broken identity. If on the other hand he has been linked by faith to Jesus he will experience not only judgment but also true "eternal life". Like any idea about what happens in the next life, Pannenberg admits, this is only an earthly metaphor.

Hick is critical of Pannenberg's narrowness about the limited number of people who are saved, as well as the frozen and perhaps dismal state of eternity that Pannenberg seems to envision. As we shall see below, in chapter 7, Hans Küng is particularly interested in the contribution of Pannenberg on this issue.

Roger Haight

Roger Haight is a Jesuit priest, professor of historical and systematic theology at Weston School of Theology in Cambridge, Massachusetts, and author of *Jesus Symbol of God*.[2] He has a chapter on "Jesus' Resurrection" which provides for Christians a model of their own resurrection and in the process gives a good view of contemporary Catholic theological anthropology. Haight's thinking on this subject is not merely his own but depends on many other contemporary theologians and reflects their understanding, for example Xavier Leon-Dufour,[3] John Galvin,[4] Gerald O'Collins,[5] Reginald H. Fuller,[6] Kenan B. Osborne[7] and Karl Rahner.[8] All of these authors do not share exactly the same opinion of Haight but can be considered "fellow travelers".

Haight recalls that before the Enlightenment and nineteenth century historical criticism the traditional understanding of the resurrection of Jesus was literal: life was restored to Jesus' dead body by the power of God. Today a modern liberal interpretation is that Jesus did not really rise from the dead but lives on in the faith of the Christian community. Neither of these interpretations represent either the historical fact or the meaning of Christ's resurrection as it is reported in the New Testament. Haight proposes one way to understand in a reasonable way today the meaning of "Christ is risen".

The New Testament records the resurrection of Christ in two ways. Both tell us that Jesus did not remain under the power of death but is alive, and both say this with different emphases. One describes his resurrection as an awakening or a rising from physical death (e.g.. Acts 2, 32; Acts 10, 39-41; Luke 24, 34). The other describes it as an "exaltation" or "glorification", so that after his death Jesus is in a state of glory; he is Lord (e.g. Acts 2, 33; 1 Tim. 3; Phil. 2, 6-11). Four things need to be said about these New Testament texts.

1) The early disciples believed that Jesus was really alive, raised and exalted in glory with God (not merely in the faith of the community but really.)

2) His resurrection was not a return to life in this world (not a resuscitation of his corpse) and is not limited by or contained in the space-time continuum. Rather it was a passage into another sphere, the sphere of the ultimate and absolute reality which is the Creator himself. This reality is not another creation but transcends all creation without being altogether unrelated to it. This was not an empirical event and only in this sense it was not an historical fact. But it can be known by us with faith-hope.

3) His resurrection was an exaltation and glorification of the whole individual person Jesus of Nazareth, so that the personal identity of Jesus during his lifetime in this world and his being with God is continuous.

4) His life after resurrection is transcendent, i.e. in another order of reality than space-time, namely outside of all creation with the life of the creating God.

After all this Haight summarizes his own belief in these words:

In sum what is the nature of the resurrection? It is the assumption of Jesus of Nazareth into the life of God. It is Jesus being exalted and glorified within God's reality. This occurred through and at the moment of Jesus' death, so that there was no time between death and his resurrection and exaltation. This is a transcendent reality which can only be appreciated by faith-hope. I take this to be a middle and mediating position between existentialist and empirical-historicist interpretation of the New Testament witness.

Haight also gives us two very useful principles that need to be used in any attempt to understand the resurrection of Jesus (and I would add, to any attempt to understand the "resurrection of the dead" promised to men in the ancient Christian creeds.)

One is that in our interpretations we should avoid speculation that includes things that today are proven to be impossible. The other is that we must be careful of our imaginations; they are dangerous in an area where we have no evidence and can easily lead us into absurdities.

Hans Küng

Hans Küng, director of the Institute for Ecumenical Research at the University of Tübingen, in his book *Eternal Life?*[9] reveals his theological anthropology in his analysis of "Resurrection".

First, he says, the resurrection of Jesus was not an historical event. "Christ is risen" is a theological assertion, not an historical one. It is not an event that occurred in space and time. It is not a miraculous occurrence achieved by the supernatural intervention of God contradicting or suspending the laws of nature. It was not a public verifiable event that could be photographed or in some other way objectively certified. Neither is it, on the other hand, merely an event imagined, made up, or wished for. Nor is it merely an event that lives on only in the minds and memory of others, or lives on in a subsequent movement or cause that carries on his ideas and purposes, while he himself is no longer really alive.

Rather the resurrection of Jesus was a real event that actually occurred. It was the entering of Jesus into God's life beyond space and time. It is God's victory over death freely given to a man, the entrance of Jesus through the power of God into a new mode of existence, a transcendental sphere, spaceless and timeless.

This real event is not historical evidence of anything and does not cause faith. It is rather a call to and offer of faith, a free decision on our part of something that actually occurred, cannot be proven but is not unreasonable. It is possible for a person to say, "Death is the end of everything for everyone. We all die like animals. There is nothing afterwards." If a person chooses to say this, he cannot be refuted on rational or empirical grounds. But it is also possible for a person to say; "Death is not the end of everything. Through the power and love of God there can be something more." This statement too cannot be refuted on purely rational or empirical grounds.

Küng does not leave the matter there. He reminds us that St. Paul said that Jesus is the first fruit, the first to be raised from the dead. Resurrection of the body is a gift from God not only to Christ but to everyman. But Küng asks, how do we picture or describe this? Küng's answer is: "Not at all."

All our images or descriptions here are necessarily only metaphors, efforts to describe with things that we have experienced other things that we have not and can not experience now. "There are things which no eye ever saw and no ear ever heard, and never occurred to the human mind which God has provided for those who love him."[10]

Our eyes, ears, imaginations cannot help here; they can only mislead us. This new resurrected life is beyond our imagination, vision and language. It is something we can hope for but not picture or describe. There are areas where physicists have a similar problem, for instance in describing light in the atomic and sub-atomic fields with metaphors of waves, corpuscles, and intangible mathematical formulae. St. Paul had the same problem in all his efforts to describe with metaphors what is finally inexpressible.

At this point in his essay Küng comes directly to the issue that we are exploring—the relationship of the body and soul in human beings. Küng says, "When Paul speaks of resurrection, what he means is simply not the Greek idea of the immortality of a soul that has to be freed from the prison of the mortal body. *The body-soul problem* as a whole must be judged extremely critically in the light of biblical theology.

Küng notes that the Protestant theologian Paul Althaus rightly insists in his book, *The Last Things: A Textbook of Eschatology*, that Christian faith generally speaks, "not of immortality of the soul, but of immortality, indissolubility of the personal relationship with God; but this affects man in the totality of his mental-bodily existence. It is not a question of the 'soul' but of the person as a living unit of corporeal-mental being founded by God's call."

Küng adds that another Protestant theologian, Wolfhart Pannenberg, got the whole matter right when he said that the human person is no longer thought of as "constructed from two quite different materials". The separation of mental and corporeal behavior is artificial. The body and soul cannot be distinguished into two different realities. "It follows," Küng says, "that there is not an independent reality known as 'soul' in man as opposed to 'body', any more than there is a purely mechanical or unconsciously moving body. Both are abstractions. What is real is solely the unity of the self-moving living being, man, in his behavior in regard to the world."

After a person's death, Küng concludes, it is this same unity, the very same human corporeal person that he was in this life, the *soma* in the biblical sense, that enters into the new life with God in a glorified state adapted to the new transcendent state of timelessness and spacelessness. His old physical body, his corpse or "remains", decays as the mere earthly molecules that they now are.

This is the substance of Hans Küng's thought on the nature of man, and nothing could be clearer. However, in a later chapter in the same book, he introduces a new problem, one which appears in papal documents. The chapter is entitled, "Between Heaven and Hell"

In this chapter, which discusses hell, Küng recalls that in 1215 the Fourth Lateran Council "without passing judgment on individuals but clearly affirming collective guilt declared whole gigantic groups of people (in practice all non-Catholics) to be damnable: 'The Holy Roman Church . . . firmly believes, professes and proclaims that none of those outside the Catholic Church, not Jews, nor heretics, nor schismatics, can participate in eternal life, but will go into the eternal fire prepared for the devil and his angels, unless they are brought into [the Catholic Church] before the end of life'."[11]

Immediately after this Küng adds that Catholics too may be
sentenced to the same fire according the general disposition of
Benedict XII in 1336: "We define that according to the general
disposition of God the souls of those who die in actual mortal sin
go down immediately after death into hell and are there tormented
by the pains of hell."[12]

Küng then notes that in 1964 the Second Vatican Council, without expressly admitting it, effectively took back the teaching of the
Fourth Lateran Council by teaching that even atheists in good faith
can attain eternal salvation.[13]

What catches one's attention is the definition by Pope Benedict
XII, which is wedged in between the teaching of the Fourth Lateran
and the Second Vatican councils. The pope says that the souls who
die in mortal sin go straight to hell after death. Therefore it can be
concluded that for the pope, as for Plato, the human soul is sepa-
rable from the human body. But Küng lets this definition pass without comment. It is also interesting that Karl Rahner under "Resurrection of the Flesh" in his *Theological Dictionary* cites the other
part of Pope Benedict's definition: "Against his predecessor John
XXII, Benedict XII defined the dogma that the human animating
principle may attain the beatific vision even before its fulfillment in
glorified corporeality and need not await the resurrection of the
flesh."[14]

The background behind Benedict's famous Constitution
Benedictus Deus is an intriguing piece of history. If the reader is
interested he can find it detailed by Jaroslav Pelican in the fourth
volume of his *The Christian Tradition*.[15] The short of the story is
this. During the sojourn of the popes in Avignon and amid much
political and civil unrest Benedict's predecessor, Pope John XXII
who had already been accused of heresy, taught in a sermon that
separated souls are not given the beatific vision until after the resurrection of their bodies. After the resulting turmoil (Poulet-Raemers
says, "at the point of death") he retracted his teaching in the pres-
ence of his cardinals. Afterwards, to put an end to the controversy,
Benedict XII issued his apostolic constitution.

The reason Küng passed over Benedict's definition without comment, I suspect, is that it is clear from the historical context that the point of the definition was not to settle the issue of whether or not souls can exist separately from their bodies. That they can was the tacit assumption of both popes but not the object of Benedict's definition. What precisely was in dispute and so was the point of the definition was the timing of eternal reward or punishment: when did it start, immediately after a person's death or not until the last and general judgment? In Küng's mind both popes were wrong, but we are not confronted with any dogma here.

What is more, since timing was the object of the papal definition, and if the pope is right, he confirmed Küng's thesis that the "resurrection" of man (*soma*) occurs right after his death, and he does not have to wait for a universal resurrection of all men and a general judgment at the end of time.

There is one thing more. As the Ascension of Jesus into heaven does not describe a journey of Jesus into space but is merely another aspect of resurrection, so the descent of Jesus into hell is not a journey of Jesus' soul in another direction. Küng explains that this article in the Apostles' Creed did not appear in the creed until the fourth century, is not clearly related to anything in scripture, and has had various interpretations at various times in Christian history. Most likely it was simply a statement of Jesus' fate in death, which was often understood as Jesus' victory over death and Satan. It certainly did not indicate or suppose an intermediate time between Jesus' death and resurrection. In his *Theological Dictionary* Rahner confirms this, saying that *Descent into Hell* in the Apostles' Creed "is simply Christ being dead."

Karl Rahner, S. J.

The theological anthropology of Karl Rahner is widely spread throughout his writings on eschatology, death, resurrection, life, humanization, natural science, et. al. The most complete and systematic treatment of the matter is in his essay titled "The Unity of Spirit and Matter in the Christian Understanding of Faith".[16] *Chris-*

tian is deliberately put in the title of this article to indicate that this essay "is neither a controversial subject disputed among the Christian denominations, nor a properly philosophical investigation . . ." It is the understanding of the Christian faith.

There exists today, Rahner says, a worldwide materialism which disputes the very foundations of the Christian faith. We cannot simply hide our heads in the sand, pretending that every question raised by materialists today already has been completely worked out and answered in the past. We have the duty to think anew on all these questions, to face up to the new attitudes of the men of our times and assimilate into our theological understanding whatever we can, simply because it is true. There are, of course, Christians who have made up their minds on nearly every question and therefore will see our efforts as a dangerous concession to our opponent. They feel that the only proper and useful attitude to materialism is a bitter and solid contraction of it.

Christian theology, of course, must be wary of any lazy compromises with false philosophical systems, the spirit of the age, or the powers of evil. But we must not close ourselves in with the unchristian spirit of some of the earlier centuries and refuse to learn anything more.

In the Christian understanding, matter is not the enemy of spirit or the principle of evil as some religions believed in the past. There is no radical dualism between matter and spirit. On the contrary, Christians believe that in this world matter and spirit have one origin, one history and one destiny.

This means that the Christian faith believes that the spirit did not exist before matter, that it forms one unified being with matter, and that at death it is not set free from matter but rather that the dead body by a "resurrection of the flesh" somehow, in an unimaginable way, also survives extinction, so that the "whole man composed of matter and spirit" attains his perfection and ultimate destiny. Therefore, in man matter and spirit do not exist one beside the other but form one unified thing and are irreversibly related to each other.

From this explanation one wonders what exactly Rahner means by *matter* and *spirit*. Do these words simply name different aspects of the same reality or do they designate different things united to form one reality?

Rahner tells us that matter and spirit, although they form one and the same reality, are not identical. Spirit is not a product of matter or something that can be derived from it. The Church, he says, has never defined this but supposes it as already known.

Rahner wants to insist on a difference between spirit and matter without falling into some form of dualism. Hence his distinction between matter and spirit is up to this point, if not unintelligible, at least subtle.

But before any attempt to distinguish matter from spirit, he says, it might be useful to establish the meaning that one attaches to the words. Of any absolute materialist—one who says that nothing exists except matter—ask, "What is matter?" Then, Rahner says, ask him, "What is spirit?" which he reduces to matter.

If he gives a metaphysical answer, that matter is the same thing as being, the answer is not a univocal definition but an analogical one, since matter is then an analogical idea which applies to every reality in a different way. More likely he will give a scientific answer, saying something like "matter consists in purely empirical data, which is experienced and ordered by mathematicised functional relationships". But the truth is that even in modern science matter is a far deeper mystery than that.

Spirit, on the other hand, is "an a priori datum of human knowledge". For, Rahner explains, the first object that man experiences subjectively is himself, that is the unified being that he is. This, of course, Rahner concedes, "requires a further interpreting reflex articulation".

This text leaves the reader puzzled about Rahner's understanding and definition of the "spirit" that is mixed with matter in man. The truth is that the precise meanings that Rahner attaches to either *matter* or *spirit* are not disclosed in this context.

In another context Rahner says that the difference between matter and spirit is certainly not an absolute metaphysical separation of the two realities, and it does not necessarily imply that "there can be objects in the world that can be absolutely and in every respect exempt from the material laws which we discover in our empirically experienced reality of a material kind."

The essential difference between matter and spirit is one of priority. This does not mean, of course, that the human spirit in any way preexisted its body, or even that spirit is better to the extent that it is distanced from matter. It only means that the spirit or its meaning cannot be deduced from matter. On the contrary, God "transcends this intramundane distinction of spirit and matter." He created matter for spirit, not spirit for matter. In fact, it is doubtful that God could create a world that was only material, since that would be quite meaningless. All of man's material reality is "the reality and expression of his spirit". At the same time spirit enters so deeply into matter that the spirit comes at that moment into the fullness of its being.

The spiritual soul, precisely as spiritual, Rahner says, is the form of the body. The "finite spirit searches for and finds itself through the fulfillment of the material itself and is so close to matter that matter is a factor of its own becoming as a spirit, of its becoming-conscious-of-itself, viz. in man". Therefore in man matter must be understood spiritually and spirit must be materialized. Rahner summarizes:

> Thus the Christian can only really be a materialist and a spiritualist at the same time if these two words are not ultimately referring to particular regions of the total reality, regions which lie side by side, but refer to factors which wherever encountered, though essentially different, are everywhere correlative constitutive moments of the one reality.

There is one other closely related issue that Rahner discusses in this essay, a question about the evolution of man and the human spirit. The average theological interpretation today is that the human spirit is not the product of natural development and evolution but is directly created by God in each instance by a new creative intervention. But, Rahner says, this is not necessarily so.

God is the creator of everything in the sense that he is the transcendent ground of all existence but not in the sense that he is the direct and immediate cause of every individual thing. God usually works indirectly through "secondary causes".

To say that matter evolved over a long period of time into a body ready to receive a spiritual form unnecessarily introduces a new type or appearance of dualism. Becoming in itself is not limited to a change only on one level of being. It is possible for a thing to become something new, to go beyond itself by surpassing its nature. This is "true self-transcendence not merely a passive being surpassed".

Accordingly, a development of matter in the direction of the spirit is not an impossible notion, presupposing merely that the notion of development is understood in the sense of that essential self-transcendence under the dynamism of the absolute being.[17]

So far Rahner is insistent in avoiding any form or appearance of dualism in his explanation of the makeup of man. He will complete his explanation and develop a full and coherent anthropology in his discussion of eschatology.

Rahner's Eschatology

In a brief article, originally given as a lecture in 1960 and titled, "The Hermeneutics of Eschatological Assertions",[18] Rahner sets out a principle in interpreting eschatological images used in scripture and popular preaching, art and writing.

The eschata, he says, are by definition future and hidden mysteries. Popular images and images used in Sacred Scripture (e.g. coming of Christ on the clouds of heaven, the sound of trumpets, the opening of graves, a gathering in the valley of Jehosophat, stars falling, being carried up in the air to meet Christ, the general conflagration, etc.) not only cannot realistically be harmonized with each other but never were intended to realistically describe the eschaton. These images cannot be used to support a pseudo-Christian apocalyptic. All that a true Christian eschatology knows from such images is that Christ's salvation is present in the world and he will surely complete and perfect his mission of redeeming the world.

A short 1959 article on the Resurrection of Christ gives a clue to the direction that Rahner's eschatology will take.[19] Rahner notes that dogmatic theology has been impoverished in this area because in the last century the task of studying the resurrection of Jesus was taken over by apologetics, whose job was to defend Christianity against attacks from outside. What was worse, Western theology in general took mainly a juridical approach to interpreting the resurrection of Jesus, emphasizing the idea of satisfaction for sin. This was true for both Catholics and Protestants, not only in their theology but also in their preaching and liturgy. A good example of this is Rudolph Bultman who in his writings looks away from Easter to concentrate on the role of the cross in our redemption.

The death and resurrection of Jesus needs to be reflected on in itself, since it is the model of our own death and resurrection. Death, he says, is not simply the separation of the soul and the body. The death of Christ and his resurrection must be seen as two aspects of a "strictly unitary event." These two aspects are essentially related to each other as the "handing over of the whole bodily man to the mystery of the merciful loving God." "This," Rahner says, "is Easter, and the redemption of the world."

Rahner continues this idea and applies it to human beings in general in an article on eschatology titled "Immanent and Transcendent Consummation of the World".[20] In this article Rahner emphasis that human death must not be interpreted as the "dividing" of the spiritual soul from matter. This is implicit in the Christian dogma of the substantial unity of spirit and matter in man.[21] Rahner explains:

> . . . man's personal history as spiritual being is identical with his material and biological life (it does not preexist this, nor is the soul sojourning" in an alien setting, nor does it have any further and separate history of its own after death).

Thus, the essential difference between spirit and matter in man begins to become clear. Spirituality and materiality are different only in so far as they are the metaphysical principles of one single "spiritual-material being". Matter, which is the materiality of the spirit, is itself spiritual in as much as it is an intrinsic co-principle in a spiritual and personal being and shares in its final destiny. Rahner realizes that time ends for man after his death. Therefore not only does the soul not preexist the body; it does not have to "wait around for a while" until the resurrection of its body.

Moreover, if matter in man can be said to be spiritual, so can the human spirit be called material. In an earlier article on this topic called "The Resurrection of the Body" Rahner described the resurrection as the perfection of the whole man before God, giving him eternal life. The resurrection of the body is not secondary or incidental to the "immortality of the soul" as theologians infected by Platonism thought. For "the personal spirit, precisely as human spirit, is a material, mundane, incarnate—indeed *intra*mundane spirit".[22]

In a 1981 article entitled "Natural Science and Reasonable Faith" Rahner applied his ideas on spirit and matter to some of the relevant issues of contemporary natural science. His ideas do not differ from what he said in his more abstract or detached writings. But here his purpose seems to be to reassure some conservative Christians (perhaps also the Holy See) that we can no longer hold on stubbornly to ideas of the past and that these new ideas, which are more compatible with the ideas of contemporary science, do not put in jeopardy divine revelation or the substance of Christian faith.[23]

Rahner's ideas on death appear in a few other articles, some more thorough than others. One rather brief article is "The Life of the Dead".[24] Here Rahner says plainly that death is the end of the *whole* man, the end of everything for him, since after his death time does not really go on for him. That is why in the Christian faith in its orthodox sense the expressions "immortality of the soul" and "resurrection of the flesh" must refer to the same reality—the whole man in his unified being.

(Incidentally, in an effort to make sense in this context of the Catholic doctrine of purgatory Rahner suggests that in this timeless state one can distinguish two phases—the definitive finality of man and his full perfection which is achieved by his basic decision penetrating the whole extent of his reality).[25]

In a 1958 essay called "Zur Theologie des Todes, Freiburg."[26] Rahner is again critical of the common definition of death as the separation of the soul and the body. This is not an adequate definition; it is neither a biblical nor an essential definition. It may be a proper definition of death for an animal or man on the sheer biological level, but it does not describe human death. Human death is an event for man as a whole, as a spiritual person. It is man, the whole man, who dies.

What is more, at death man's soul does not continue to exist unrelated to matter; it does not become "a-cosmic" but in some way "pancosmic", i.e. related to all matter in the world. This idea was severely criticized by John Hick and others as "highly speculative" and "wholly obscure".[27] It represented an early and unsuccessful effort of Rahner to avoid any platonic interpretation of the human soul. Rahner never repeated this idea again.

In a later analysis of death in 1970, "Ideas for a Theology of Death"[28] Rahner insists that at death man does not continue to live on simply by "changing horses" as Feuerbach thought, Rather man as such no longer exists in time or space. There is no temporal interval between his death and his resurrection. In fact, statements like "continued existence of the soul after death", "the soul's separation from the body", and "resurrection of the body" for him are statements about "one and the same state of affairs" which is pointed to by different conceptual models.

Contemporary physics, he notes, sometimes has to do the same thing. For instance it uses different and seemingly contradictory conceptual models like particles or waves to explain one and the same thing. It should be no surprise that we must do the same when stammering about a matter that lies entirely beyond our experience.

In 1976 Rahner repeated and expanded these ideas in the eschatology section of his *Foundations of Christian Faith*.[29]

Chapter Eight

Conclusion

The Hebrew mind did not think in terms of spiritual souls. Hebrews only understood man—one material being specially created by their God. The authors of the New Testament had the same understanding. *Spirit* (πνεῦμα) is used in the New Testament, especially by St. Paul, not to designate another natural immaterial component of a human being. Rather it names a new supernatural gift or grace from God elevating man into the supernatural order. The authors of the Bible knew nothing of dualism, either Platonic or Cartesian. There were no ghosts in their machines.

The ancient Christian creeds continued this tradition. No creed ever professed belief in the immortality of a soul. Rather the early creeds professed belief in the resurrection of the body or resurrection of the dead. Later some Christian writers, influenced by neoplatonism, began to talk about separate spiritual substances inside of human beings.

The idea of immaterial souls was introduced into Christian thinking by Origen in the East and Augustine in the West. Origen was brilliant, the most prolific writer in the history of Christianity and perhaps in all antiquity. He ran into disciplinary and doctrinal problems with the ecclesiastical authorities of his time, made his share of errors, but exerted great doctrinal influence at a time when Christianity was beginning to formulate its faith in a thematic way.

Origen knew that many prominent Christian writers of the time believed in the materiality of human souls as an integral part of the Christian tradition. But he preferred the Greek understanding that the human soul was a spiritual substance.

In the Western part of the Church Augustine also supported the Platonic idea of the spirituality of the soul. Before he became a Christian Augustine had been a Manichean, believing that matter in itself was evil, in fact the principle of evil at war with the good. Augustine had renounced Manicheism when he accepted Christianity. But the spiritualism of Platonism must have proven a comforting contrast to his former faith.

Augustine never said that the body and soul existed apart from each other or that man is essentially a soul. But he did accept Plato's idea that the soul uses the body as its instrument and is superior to its body. But he never resolved the problem about exactly how the body and soul are united.

Augustine was a powerful figure in his day. He was both a genius and a busybody, personally concerned about all the affairs of the early Church. In his recent biography of St. Augustine Gary Wills tells of Augustine's efforts to instruct St. Jerome on the way to translate the Bible. St. Jerome, a learned monk, was retranslating the whole Bible directly from the original languages. Augustine told Jerome that that was not necessary; it would be sufficient to simply refurbish, as it were, the old extant Latin translations, so as to make texts more appealing for liturgical use in the Church. All Christians today are in debt to St. Jerome because the crotchety old monk ignored the advice of the distinguished bishop. Jerome did this not only because he was crotchety but also because Augustine, the Platonist, knew neither Hebrew nor Greek.

Augustine and Origen did not win the day even in their own time. There was vigorous opposition to the Greek idea of spiritual souls from other important Christian writers, especially in the Western part of the Church, for instance Tertullian and his disciples. Some writers conceded that the soul was like a fluid, more simple and subtle than water, but still matter. At the time there was a variety of understandings of matter (as there is among physicists today). But these early Christians still believed that (1) the soul was corporeal and (2) that fact was not in any way opposed to the personal immortality of man.

Not only did Augustine's authority last well into the middle ages. Even after the introduction of Aristotle into the new medieval universities, none of the great medieval scholastics, until St. Thomas Aquinas, dared to say plainly with Aristotle that the soul is *per se et essentialiter* the form of the body. In spite of external pressures Thomas rejected Augustine's Platonism. The soul is not a different substance, living inside the body and using it as an instrument. Man in her essence is one united being. The human soul forms with her body one substance. The soul is not merely united to the body accidentally. Rather it is an essential constituent of human nature. Despite all pressures Thomas stood firm on this. For Thomas there was no ghost in the machine.

However, for some reason Thomas did waffle in his *DeAnima*. When discussing the question of the soul's existence after death Thomas, inconsistent with Aristotelian hylomorphism, said that the soul can survive for a while until the final resurrection at which time it will be reunited with its body.

It is possible that this inconsistency may have been caused by respect for or pressure from ecclesiastical authorities. But more likely it was due to St. Thomas' own puzzlement or confusion about the best way not to put in any jeopardy the certain Christian belief in the immortality of man and the general judgment at the time of the second coming of Christ at the end of the world. In any event, while he did not expressly take back his commitment to hylomorphism, he was inconsistent with Aristotelianism here.

The immortality of man is a dogma of the Christian faith, clearly affirmed in the New Testament, official church teaching, and the constant faith of the people. But the spirituality of the soul, introduced from Greek philosophy as a polemic support of the dogma of human immortality, was never explicitly defined as such in official church teaching.

It has been assumed by Church authorities and asserted *indirecte et obiter*. But it was left at that, perhaps as one theologian suggested, because the immateriality of the soul was incidental and never as important as the doctrine that it was introduced to protect. Accordingly, seminary textbooks did not give it the kind of prominence or importance that it gave to the central dogma of the faith, that through Christ death is swallowed up in victory, that every man as a free gift of God somehow will continue to live forever.

Contemporary theological literature brings all this history into focus. Roger Haight supplies the model for thinking about resurrection in general in his analysis of the meaning of the resurrection of Jesus as it is recorded in the New Testament.

Hans Küng explains the doctrine of resurrection in much the same way as Haight. Like the resurrection of Christ man's resurrection is not a physical resuscitation but a new existence outside of space-time in a glorified body at the moment of death, while his old physical "remains" decay. Likewise Karl Rahner is insistent that there is no room for any kind of dualism in an authentic Christian understanding of man.

Rahner's explanation was an evolving one. In an early paper on the theology of death he insisted on the fundamental unity of corporeal man. She is essentially one being. But after death, when the spirit no longer forms one being with the body but cannot exist independently from matter, Rahner suggested that for a time, while the soul awaits the resurrection of its body, it has its being united to the matter of the world. This theory is not easy to make sense of, was sharply criticized by other theologians, and was never repeated by him again. It was probably a blunder because it had not yet occurred to him then, as it did in his later writings, that at death time no longer exists for man.

Nonetheless, Rahner persists in denying any form of dualism in the makeup of man. He keeps repeating that man is one unified being, which is composed of matter and spirit and that matter and spirit are not the same, and spirit cannot simply be reduced to matter as if they were identical.

Finally he explains without ambiguity that matter and spirit form in the concrete one and the same reality; on the physical level of things matter and spirit are the same thing.

The difference is on the metaphysical level. In man spirituality and materiality are different only in as much as they are the metaphysical principles of the one single spiritual-material being. In the

subsistent concrete entity matter is spiritualized and spirit materialized.

Here it appears that Rahner repairs to the metaphysics of Aristotle
and specifically to hylomorphism. The soul is the form of the body.
Body and soul are related as potency to act, and neither can exist
without the other. It is interesting to see that Rahner is free from
St. Thomas' problem of explaining the existence of the soul after
the death of the body by Rahner's insight that death is the end of
everything for the whole man, since after death time no longer
exists for him.

One interpretation of Rahner's circumlocutions is that at the
time he felt the pressure of papal authority coming from Pius XII's
encyclical letter *Humani Generis* on polygenism and the papal in-
sistence on the special creation of the individual human soul. But
now that the present pope has declared that scientific conclusions
about evolution are more than mere theory, contemporary concerns about *Humani Generis* are considerably diminished if not
forgotten.

But it is more likely that the reason for Rahner's apparent unclarity or ambiguity here is simply the explanation he himself gave,
when he said that in dealing with such opaque matters as death,
where no one is talking from any experience, it is not surprising
that in order to be as accurate as possible we sometimes need to
talk in paradoxes, saying apparently contradictory things in order
to say as much as possible about the opaque reality. Death, he says,
is something like light. To approach the reality as closely as possible physicists have to define light as both particles and waves.

From all this history the best conclusion is that man is not an
immaterial substance inhabiting a material body. She is one being,
a wholly material one, with a soul which is not more than the name
of an animating principle. That represents the purified Christian
tradition which comes, with some confusion but without interrup-
tion, from the New Testament to Christian anthropology today.

Anything more is not derived from divine revelation in the New
Testament but from Greek philosophy in the second and third centuries after Christ. This accretion was vigorously resisted by pow-

erful spokesmen for authentic Christian doctrine at the time it was introduced and later was abandoned by Christian theologians and Church teaching.

It must be said that Christianity cannot simply tailor its essential beliefs to conform to the current secular wisdom. As St. Paul said, the folly of God is wiser than the wisdom of men. But the folly of men is not wiser than the wisdom of men. We are not allowed to confuse our own human wisdom with the wisdom of God and defend the one as if it were the other.

Christians, especially Catholic Christians, do not need another Galileo case. Despite some temptations, Catholic and mainstream Protestant Christians have managed to keep their nerve over Darwin and Freud. There is no need to lose our nerve with respect to the essential definition of man and the scientific description and analysis of human consciousness. For, as we have seen, anthropological monism is the *maior et sanior pars* of the Christian tradition.

Perhaps it should be observed in conclusion that unless one is a Manichean, or an Irish Jansenist, this understanding of man does not diminish her in any way. She remains the pinnacle of God's creation. She is no less because she is made of matter. In fact, as Karl Rahner once said, she is not less than the angels because she is in her entire being matter. God made her matter; God loves matter; in fact, according to another Christian dogma, God himself became matter.

Epilogue

by Nobel Laureate Gerald M. Edelman, M.D, Ph.D. and
Neuroscientist Giulio Tononi, M.D., Ph.D.*

There is a common prejudice that to call something material is somehow to refuse its entry into the realm of exalted things— mind, spirit, pure thought. The word *material* can be used to refer to many things or states. As it is used in these pages, it applies to what we commonly call the real world of sensible or measurable things, the world that scientists study. That world is considerably more subtle than it first appears. A chair is material (shaped by us, of course), a star is material, atoms and fundamental particles are material—they are made of matter-energy. The thought "thinking about Vienna," however, while couched in material terms, is, as Willard Van Orman Quine pointed out, a materially based process but is, itself, not material.

What is the difference? It is that conscious thought is a set of relations with a meaning that goes just beyond energy or matter (although it involves both). And what of the mind that gave rise to that thought? The answer is, it is both material and meaningful. There is a material basis for the mind as a set of relations. The action of your brain and all its mechanisms, bottom to top, atoms to behavior, results in a mind that can be concerned with processes of meaning. While generating such immaterial relationships that are recognized by it and other minds, this mind is completely based in and dependent on the physical processes that occur in its own workings, in those of other minds, and in the events involved in commu-

---

* (reprinted from *A Universe of Consciousness: How Matter Becomes Imagination*: New York, 2000, with permission of Basic Books).

nication. There are no separate domains of matter and mind and no grounds for dualism. But obviously, there is a realm created by the physical order of the brain, the body, and the social world in which meaning is consciously made.

That meaning is essential both to our description of the world and to our scientific understanding of it. It is the amazingly complex material structures of the nervous system and body that give rise to dynamic mental processes and to meaning. Nothing else need be assumed—neither other worlds, or spirits, or remarkable forces as yet unplumbed, such as quantum gravity.

There is a web to untangle here: Humans were capable of meaning and of thought before they had a scientific description of the world. Any such scientific description, even when clarified, cannot be fully tested or sustained by just one person for an indefinite period of time. It needs social interactions or, at least, two persons to make an ongoing experimental science. Yet a single person can have both private thoughts, not fully capturable by a scientific description, at the same time that he or she has a quite correct scientific understating. So, what happens when we turn scientific inquiry in the direction of the individual human brain and mind? What are the limits? What can we expect to capture and understand by such a scientific adventure?

Our claim is that we may capture the material bases of mind even to the extent of having a satisfactory understanding of the origins of exalted things, such as the mental. To do so, we may have to invent further ways of looking at brains and their activities. We may even have to synthesize artifacts resembling brains connected to bodily functions in order fully to understand those processes. Although the day when we shall be able to create such conscious artifacts is far off, we may have to make them—that is use synthetic means—before we deeply understand the processes of thought itself. However far off the date of their construction, such artifacts shall be made. After all, it has been done at least once by evolution. The history of science, particularly of biological science, has shown repeatedly that apparently mysterious or impassable barriers to our understanding were based on false views or technical limitations. The material bases of mind are no exception.

This position does not contradict the conclusion that each mind is unique, not fully exhaustible by scientific means, and not a machine. Do not search for the mystical here. Our statement about the material order and immaterial meaning are not only mutually consistent within a scientific framework, but live in a useful symbiosis.

Notes

Chapter One: State of the Question

1. Philosopher David J. Chalmers in *The Conscious Mind: In Search of a Fundamental Theory* (Oxford University Press: New York, 1996) has produced a careful, thorough and subtle study of the mind-body problem in which he says that he thinks dualism is the more likely theory here. But by *dualism* he really means a nicely nuanced form of physicalism or materialism.

2. Brian Green, *The Elegant Universe: Superstrings, Hidden Dimensions, and the Quest for the Ultimate Theory* (W.W. Norton & Company: New York, 1999). Also, for a new theory of time (as well as space) see Julian Barbour, *The End of Time: The Next Revolution in Physics* (Oxford University Press: New York, 2000).

Chapter Two: Three Current Responses

1. *The Character of the Mind* (Oxford University Press: Oxford, 1997); *The Foundations of Consciousness* (Basil Bleakly: Oxford, 1991); *Problems in Philosophy* (Basil Bleakly: Oxford, 1993); *Minds and Bodies* (Oxford University Press: New York, 1997).

2. Less technical is his most recent analysis entitled *The Mysterious Flame: Conscious Minds in a Material World* (Basic Books: New York, 1999).

3. *The Large, The Small and The Human Mind* (Cambridge University Press: New York, 1997). See also Roger Penrose, *The Emperor's New Mind: Concerning Computers, Minds and the Laws of Physics* (Oxford University Press: New York, 1989); *Shadows of the Mind: An Approach to the Missing Science of Consciousness* (Oxford University Press: Oxford, 1994); Stephen Hawking and Roger Penrose, *The Nature of Space and Time* (Princeton University Press: Princeton, NJ, 1996).

4. Since this is the foundation of his argument, in addition to his thirty page discussion of the issue *The Large, The Small and the Human*

Mind Penrose dedicates the first two hundred pages of his *Shadows of the Mind* to prove it.

5. Harcourt Brace & Company: New York, 1999. An earlier book by Damasio on the same topic is *Descartes' Error: Emotion, Reason, and the Human Brain* (Avon Books: New York, 1994). Damasio mentions a number of recent studies from many disciplines and points of view, which have made useful contributions in the past few years: John Searle, *The Rediscovery of the Mind* (MIT Press: Cambridge, Mass., 1992); Patricia and Paul Churchland, *On the Contrary* (MIT Press: Cambridge, Mass., 1996; Daniel Dennett, *Consciousness Explained* (MIT Press: Cambridge, Mass., 1991); Thomas Nagel, *The View from Nowhere* (Oxford University Press: New York, 1986); Colin McGinn, *The Problem of Consciousness* (Basil Blackwell: Oxford, 1991); Owen Flanagan, *Consciousness Reconsidered* (MIT Press: Oxford, 1991). Since the release of Damasio's book an important new study, grounded in scientific experiment, by two neuroscientists has been published and should be mentioned here: Gerald M. Edelman and Guilio Tononi, *A Universe of Consciousness: How Matter Becomes Imagination* (Basic Books: New York, 2000).

Chapter Three: The Christian Sources

1. Peter Drucker, "Design and Content of Managerial Jobs," *Management* (Harper & Rowe: New York, 1974).

2. Cf. John L. McKenzie, S.J., *Dictionary of the Bible* (The Bruce Publishing Company: Milwaukee, 1965); Paul J. Achtemeier (ed.), *Harper's Bible Dictionary* (Harper & Rowe: San Francisco, 1985); James L. Mays (ed.), *Harper's Bible Commentary* (Harper & Rowe: San Francisco, 1988); Raymond E. Brown, S.S. et al. (ed.), *The New Jerome Biblical Commentary* (Prentice Hall: Englewood Cliffs, 1990); Raymond E. Brown, S.S., *An Introduction to the New Testament* (Doubleday: New York, 1997).

Chapter Four: Plato, Plotinus, and Ancient Christian Writers

1. Texts of almost all patristic writings can be found in Mingue, *Patrologiae cursus completus, Series Graeca* (162 vols. With Latin translation), (Paris, 1857-1866); and Mingue, *Patrologiae cursus completus, Series Latina* (221 vols.), (Paris, 1844-1864).

2. 3rd ed., reprint of 1929 ed.

3. *A History of Western Philosophy* (Simon and Schuster: New York, 1972).

4. PG 6.

5. PG 6.

6. PG 6.

7. PG 7.

8. PG 8-9.

9. PG 6-7.

10. Col. 2, 8.

11. PL 1-2.

12. PL 1-2. A critical edition of Tertullian's *De anima* (c. 6-9) can be found in *Corpus scriptorum ecclesiasticorum latinorum* (1906), vol. 42.

13. *The Ante-Nicene Fathers of the Church* 26, 63, 73, 131.

14. *The Ante-Nicene Fathers of the Church* 2220-222.

15. PG 44.

16. PG 40.

17. Prosper Alfaric, *L'évolution intellectuelle de saint Augustine* vol. 1 (Paris, 1919).

18. John O'Meara (ed), *Against the Academics* (Ancient Christian Writers XII: Westminster, MD, 1950).

19. There are many excellent biographies of St. Augustine. The most recent one, brief and very good, is by Gary Wills, *St. Augustine* (Viking: New York, 1999).

20. PL 32.

21. PL 32

22. For a full analysis of Augustine's anthropology see E. Dinkler, *Die Anthropolgie Augustins* (Stuttgart, 1934).

23. Etienne Gilson, "Le christianisme et la tradition philosophique", *Revue des sciences philosophiques* (1941/42) pp. 249-266.

24. *De Genesi ad lit.* PL 28.

25. William Schumacher, *Spiritus and Spiritualis: A Study in the Sermons of St. Augustine* (Mundelein, 1957).

26. PL 132.

27. PL 63-64.

28. *De Sancta Simplicitate.* PL 145-697.

Chapter Five: Aristotle, Medieval
Scholasticism, and Thomas Aquinas

1. *Quaestiones Quodlibetales* III, q. 3, a. 1.
2. *De anima* q. unica, a. 1. Cf. also a. 2 (Is the human soul separate *secundum esse*?); a. 14 (Is the human soul immoral?); a. 15 (Can the human soul separated from the body understand?). In all of these articles St. Thomas is consistent with the principle of hylomorphism that he has adopted from Aristotle: The spiritual soul is the form of the material body. At the same time Augustine is correct in saying that the spiritual soul can exist, at least for a time and awkwardly, without its body.
3. For another instance of Thomas modifying his own doctrine so as not to be in contradiction with the authority of St. Augustine (on the moral deformity of lying) see J. Dedek, "Intrinsically Evil Acts: An Historical Study of the Mind of St. Thomas," *The Thomist* 43 (1979) 385-413.

Chapter Six: Authoritative Teaching
and Prescribed Seminary Textbooks

1. *Decree on Ecumenism*, n. 74. Translation from Austin Flannery, O.P. (ed), *Vatican Council II: The Conciliar and Post Conciliar Documents*. Costello Publishing Company: Northport, 1975.
2. Cf. John F. Dedek, "Freedom of the Catholic Conscience," *McCormick Quarterly* XXII (1969) 111-120.
3. Ludwig Lercher, *Institutiones Theologicae Dogmaticae* (Herder: Innsbruck, 1951).
4. J. Dalmau, S.J. and J. Sagues, S.J., *Sacrae Thelogicae Summa* (Biblioteca De Autores Christianos: Madrid, 1964).
5. DS 902.
6. DS 1440.
7. Vol. II, p. 330-333.
8. DS 2828.
9. Vol. II p. 695-706.
10. DS 1440.
11. Vol. II, p. 695-706.
12. *The New Jerome Biblical Commentary*, p. 495.
13. *Dictionary of the Bible*, p. 838.
14. Charles Boyer, S.J., *De Deo Creante et Elevante* (Gregorian University: Rome, 1950), p. 141.

Chapter Seven: Contemporary Christian Theology

1. John Hick, *Death and Eternal Life* (Westminster/John Knox Press: Louisville, 1994).

2. *Jesus Symbol of God* (Orbis Books: New York, 1999).

3. *Resurrection and the Message of Easter* (Holt, Rinehart and Winston: New York, 1974).

4. "The Resurrection of Jesus in Contemporary Catholic Systematics," *Heythrop Journal* 20 (1979).

5. *Jesus Risen: An Historical, Fundamental and Systematic Examination of Christ's Resurrection* (Paulist Press: New York, 1987).

6. *The Formation of the Resurrection Narratives* (Fortress Press: Philadelphia, 1984).

7. *The Resurrection of Jesus: New Considerations for Its Theological Interpretation* (Paulist Press: New York, 1997).

8. "On the Theology of Hope," *Theological Investigations 10* (Herder and Herder: New York, 1973).

9. Hans Küng, *Eternal Life* (Crossroads: New York, 1996).

10. I Cor. 2, 9.

11. DS 1351.

12. DS 1002.

13. Constitution on the Church, a. 16.

14. Karl Rahner and Herbert Vorgrimler, *Theological Dictionary* (Herder and Herder: New York, 1965).

15. Jaroslav Pelican, *The Christian Tradition, vol. 4* (The University of Chicago Press: Chicago, 1984). Cf also Puolet-Raemers, *Church History* (Herder: St. Louis, 1952), and nearly all other church historians.

16. Karl Rahner, "The Unity of Spirit and Matter in the Christian Understanding of Faith," *Theological Investigations Vol. VI* (Helicon Press: Baltimore, 1969). This originally was given as a lecture in 1963 and together with some additions from his "Hominization: The Evolutionary Origin of Man as a Theological Problem", *Quaestiones Disputatae* No. 13 (Helicon Press: London, 1965) was published in 1969 under this new title.

17. The same ideas about the essential difference and real identity of spirit and matter in man were expressed by Rahner in a German article published in 1958 and in 1965 translated into English as "Hominisation: the Evolutionary Origin of Man as a Theological Problem".

18. *Theological Investigations IV* (Helicon Press: Baltimore, 1966).

19. "Dogmatic Questions on Easter," *Theological Investigations IV* (Helicon Press: Baltimore, 1969).

20. *Theological Investigations 10* (Darton, Longman & Todd: London, 1973).

21. In "Hermeneutics of Eschatological Assertions," *Theological Investigations IV* (Helicon Press: Baltimore, 1966) Rahner explains this in the technical language of hylomorphism:

> "Man consists of 'body and soul'. But in Thomistic metaphysics . . . one is bound to say that man consists of *materia prima* and of *anima* as *unica forma* and *actualitas* of this *materia prima*, so that 'body' already implies the informing of the 'soul' and hence is not another part of man beside the soul. And body and soul, if the doctrine of *anima-forma-corporis* is really understood and taken seriously, are two *meta*physical principles of one single being, and not two beings, each of which could be met with experimentally. However, even if we prescind from all this, we must at any rate affirm that every *assertion* about the body (as the reality of man) implies an assertion about the soul, and vice versa . . . If these obvious matters are not borne in mind in all anthropological assertions, 'body' and 'soul' are taken to be two entities which are only subsequently combined in unity—a unity which cannot then be really substantial; and though one may verbally profess the philosophical and dogmatic doctrine of the soul as the form of the body, one has really lost sight of it, though the soul is the form of the body by its inmost essence and is so in order *to be spirit*".

22. *Theological Investigations II* (Helicon Press: Baltimore, 1963).

23. *Theological Investigations XXI* (Helicon Press: Baltimore, 1988).

24. *Theological Investigations IV* (Helicon Press: Baltimore, 1966).

25. A fuller discussion of the question can be found in Rahner's essay on "Purgatory," *Theological Investigations XIX* (Crossroad: New York, 1983).

26. The English translation was published as "On the Theology of Death," *Quaestiones Disputatae* (Herder and Herder: New York, 1961).

27. Cf. *Death and Eternal Life*, pp. 231-235.

28. *Theological Investigations XIII* (The Seabury Press: New York, 1975).

29. The Seabury Press: New York, 1978.

30. For an analysis of Cardinal Ratzinger's understanding of this see Bernard P. Prusak, "Bodily Resurrection in Catholic Perspectives," *Theological Studies* 61 (2000) 64-105.

About the Author

John F. Dedek, a priest of the Archdiocese of Chicago, received his doctorate in theology in 1958, taught theology at St. Mary of the Lake Seminary in Mundelein, IL. and at the Catholic University of America in Washington, D.C. He was associate editor of *Chicago Studies* since its beginning in 1962, has written seven books and numerous articles in scholarly journals, and was pastor of a parish in suburban Elk Grove, IL.

We mourn his passing away in early December 2000.

Other Books by John F. Dedek

Intrinsic Evil: The Invention of an Idea

Contemporary Medical Ethics

Titius and Bertha Ride Again: Contemporary Moral Cases

Human Life: Some Moral Cases

Contemporary Sexual Morality

Experimental Knowledge of the Indwelling Trinity